Decisions Without Mistakes

(Common Sense Decision-Making Strategies for Today's Managers and Leaders)

Kim D. Ward

Writers Advantage
New York   Lincoln   Shanghai

Decisions Without Mistakes
(Common Sense Decision-Making Strategies for Today's Managers and Leaders)

Writers Advantage
an imprint of iUniverse, Inc.

For information address:
iUniverse
2021 Pine Lake Road, Suite 100
Lincoln, NE 68512
www.iuniverse.com

ISBN: 0-595-25866-2 (Pbk)
ISBN: 0-595-65392-8 (Cloth)

Printed in the United States of America

The Power of Knowledge

By: Kim D. Ward

When mornings appear to some my friends,
To be dismal, bleak or cold;
I see the challenges of the day,
As wonders about to unfold.
When others beg for borrowed time,
To face their mounting fears;
I relish the moments' warm embrace,
Recalling wisdom gained in previous years.
I know of people drowning in,
Their problems of the day;
They speak of misfortune, luck and fate.
If only they could hear me say,
I receive new hope, each morning fresh,
More glorious than the day before,
With the special gift that knowledge brings,
Great promise to my door!

Acknowledgements and Dedication

When I look back on the hours of work, the numerous conversations, consulting appointments and the hundreds of meetings that went into this little book I find myself feeling extremely blessed.

So many people have enriched my life and this book and I want you to know that I will be eternally grateful to each of you for all of your support, and understanding. Even if you're not listed here, please believe that I feel overwhelmingly fortunate to have received your assistance.

These were some of the most helpful influences:

To my family, especially my wife Robin, who put up with me being locked in my office for days and supported me unconditionally with their love, faith and confidence.

To Thomas Cooke who has shown me by example what it means to be a true caring consulting professional. And who has supported me, and the writing of this book with input, knowledge, and experience.

To Alex who gave me the chance to begin my consulting career and provided me with opportunities that I believe no one else would have offered.

To my friend J., who offered all of his expertise and his friendship without reservation.

To Dr. Bill who helped me to truly understand the benefits of looking at things a little differently.

To my mother who nurtured and developed me with a level of love, wisdom and understanding that I am still learning to appreciate.

And to all of the professionals that have offered me so many insights and experiences in every workshop and meeting.

I thank you all and dedicate this work to you!

Table of Contents

Foreword

I was honored when Kim D. Ward asked me to review his book. We have known each other for a number of years, and it has been my pleasure to share numerous speaking engagements with him. He is always entertaining, energetic, enthusiastic, and most importantly enlightening. I can assure you that you will find these characteristics throughout this book.

The compelling reason to spend your valuable time with a business-related book is to gain more than you invest. I can promise you that you will gain much from this straight forward, easy-to-follow guide for making better, daily, management decisions.

Within the book, Kim takes tough situations all managers and leaders face and blends common sense, real-life examples, humor, and his desire to help into a wonderful flow of wisdom that should be common practice. But, he doesn't stop there. He has strategically placed exercises throughout the book to assist each reader in their personal improvement journey.

I encourage each of you to pick this book up, read it, and begin your journey. Good luck. And thank you, Kim, for providing such a grassroots management book.

William D.S. Smitley, Ph.D.

Introduction

I've been in management, leadership, supervision, and directorship… whatever everyone is calling it this week, all of my adult life. You may work in the same capacity. Whether we were appointed, anointed, or the last person standing it makes no difference, the responsibilities of the job are the same. We're expected to be successful with our team. Our life, as soon as we're handed this responsibility, can become an ongoing barrage of meetings, telephone calls, e-mails, paperwork, reports, customer complaints, issues, concerns and downright problems. Isn't management/ leadership supposed to be a promotion and honor? Wow!

Why do we do it? I believe that there are a number of good answers to that question. One such answer is that many of us are successful at it! Other answers that I've heard are: "I'm the best person for the job", "I've been here the longest", "I wanted to move up", and some believe that management is a destiny, the job that they were meant to do! What ever your reason, I applaud your decision to be a manager.

A gentleman in one of my workshops said, "If it was easy… everybody would want to do it!" A young woman that was a relatively new manager quickly followed his statement with, "The real truth is that if we knew ahead of time what we were getting into…no one would want to do it!" That comment drew a healthy laugh from the group.

I believe that somewhere along the line of our lives something changes in us. And, whatever our reason at the time, we chose to accept the responsibility.

Then after we get the job, without fair warning, and in most cases with very little training the questions start coming in. "Look out! They're after me!" We find out very quickly that any real success that we wish to achieve on the job is going to be enhanced or hindered by the decisions that we are going to make. Have you ever noticed that decisions are like *boomerangs* that *always* come back? As I often suggest to the participants in my workshops, it's easy to tell the good decisions from the bad ones. Experience says that we are more likely to be held responsible for the bad decisions.

I've spent the last 10 years working with thousands of managers in a variety of industries. I've done this in workshops and consulting environments working with 15-50 managers at a time. I'm proud to say that I've learned a lot from all of those successful people.

I've also learned that the two most popular options in learning to do something well are either, the experience of trial and error (working through it yourself), or find someone who already knows how to do it well and then, do what they do. When given a choice, I choose the second option. This book is a very small distillation of some of the common sense principles, attitudes, strategies and techniques that thousands of successful people and colleges have helped me develop during my career as a trainer and consultant. We've witnessed, researched and experienced the ever-changing work environment and the outcome has been a management/leadership process that has proven to work effectively in today's interesting and challenging business setting. This book reviews part of that process.

The content of these pages can help any manager develop better business relationships, build more powerful teams, achieve higher goals, reduce stress in themselves and others, and most importantly make... **Decisions Without Mistakes!**

Enjoy and God Bless,
Kim D. Ward

Chapter One

The Consequence Factor

Our decisions have consequences! Is this true? What about the decision not to make a decision? Does it have consequences? As thousands of successful managers will attest, of course it does. As parents we attempt to teach this lesson to our children, "All decisions have consequences." In management, like in life, *our decisions determine our destiny!* I call this the *Consequence Factor.*

The Consequence Factor is the outcome of our decisions. Every time we make a management decision there will be outcomes or consequences that we must enjoy or endure because of that decision. Fortunately, some of the more unpleasant consequences take a while to get back to us. Unfortunately, some of them don't! Most of us have natural filters in our head that helps us to sift out the inappropriate or ineffective decisions before we make them public. Some of these filters are: experience, values, and just good old common sense.

Have you ever started to pass on a decision that you've made and then almost by magic stopped yourself from saying it because somehow you just knew that it wasn't the right thing to do? That was your consequence filter. Why is it then that we can sometimes with the best intentions make decisions, and have them turn out so badly?

I offer this thought, *you don't know, what you don't know.* Many of the managers with whom I've trained and consulted with over the years are

1

some of the best people I've ever met. As I'm sure you are. I can honestly say that in all my travels I have never met a manager who made conscious attempts to make the *worst* possible decisions. Although, I'm sure that somewhere in the world there are employees that believe that their manager is staying awake at night inventing new ways to make them miserable. On the contrary, I believe that every one of these people have attempted to make the *best* possible decisions that they could, with the information that they had available, in the time that they had to do it, and for the people involved. Still, we can't ignore the obvious Consequence Factor. All decisions have consequences and some of them, without the appropriate information, no matter how good the intention, turn out badly.

These poor consequences have a real and sometimes significantly negative impact on the managers, their staff, and their customers. I've had the privilege and opportunity to work with many managers in recent years, and they have helped me to create a list of the most common management decision-making mistakes that are found in the workplace today. This is that list.

Top 10 Decision Making Mistakes

1. Reacting to reoccurring problems or issues in repetitive ways.
2. Ineffectively managing change in the business or marketplace.
3. Making decisions using *ineffective* or *shifting* priorities.
4. Expecting appropriate or effective behavior from staff members without reasonable guidelines.
5. Not confronting inappropriate behavior appropriately.
6. Making decisions without vision.
7. Expecting reasonable staff member improvement without effective coaching.

8. Being in conflict with other departments.
9. Turning good employees into ex-employees.
10. Believing that *Leadership* is about encouraging *other people* to do something.

There are others, but for the purposes of this book, these 10 are the primary decision making mistakes that will be the focus and provide a good solid foundation for further discussion.

How did these get to be the top 10 Decision Mistakes? That's easy. Talk to managers about the common issues and concerns that they have today and trace them back to the root causes. Bingo…the Top 10!

In the following chapters we will take a close look at the Situations, Decisions, Complications, Consequences and Strategies for each of these Top 10 Decision Mistakes.

But first, we need to take a little closer look at the man or woman in the mirror. "Who me?" says you. "Yes you."

Let's get started!

Chapter Two

An Enlightening Reflection

There's a marvelous change that's covering the land,
Further than the eye can see.
And the thing I find most enlightening,
Is how it all began first with me!
K.D. Ward

In our management/ leadership workshops and seminars I've met many high-powered, professional, and successful adults. Many of who, I'm sure, would much rather be located somewhere else on the first morning of class. "It's not like any of my problems are going to get better or go away because I'm here for the next few days!" one manager said to me at the start of a workshop. "Can't you just e-mail me this stuff?" another asked and laughed. I then replied, as I've offered to so many others, "Lot's of managers attend seminars and workshops. They all have a million things that they could be doing. Instead, they're in class. We live in a fast paced, hurry up and get the job done world. With that in mind, many managers come to class with their business plates literally heaping over the sides with concerns, issues and responsibilities." They say, "Just tell me how to put the fix on *them*, (meaning their staff), and let me get back to work!" "Unfortunately," I say, "it just doesn't work that way."

Those of you that are parents, consider this. Have you ever read a book, watched a video, attended a class, or watched a television program about parenting? Of course you have. Why do we do that? Obviously, because we love our children and we want to become better parents. Yes? But why is that important? What are the implications of becoming a better parent? We hope that by becoming a better parent we'll then develop better children.

Those of you that have participated in organized sports of one kind or another consider this: If a coach wants to develop a better team then they must become a better coach. Doesn't this approach make sense?

The same principles apply to managers on the job. If we want better employees, we must become a better manager. That may mean making decisions differently.

Let's not lose sight of the fact that you're already successful. I mentioned that I've worked with many high-powered, professional, and *successful* adults. You should be proud of anything and everything that you've accomplished so far. Celebrate your success and enjoy your accomplishments. In my mind, if you weren't already successful and if you didn't have your business sights set on even more success, you wouldn't be reading this book. So, you're already successful. Why then should we make improvement?

Two facts are realistically clear in business today. First, everything seems to be changing. Things seem to change dramatically and quickly. Secondly, there's always room for improvement. If a person looks long enough and deeply enough, even a successful person will find reasonable room for improvement. This is one of the mindsets that successful people use to create *long-term* success. Successful people look for opportunities to make improvements, even when things are going well. Allow me to explain it this way:

I grew up in a family of four boys. I had no sisters. Some of you may know what that's like. Others may be able to imagine. Do you feel sorry for my mother yet? She worried, as I'm sure most mothers do, that something might go wrong for one of her boys. Somewhere along the way she must have decided that if she challenged us mentally that maybe we'd be better off later in life. She would ask us questions in an attempt to get us to think, or, she would offer thought provoking statements that she undoubtedly hoped would give us reason to ponder more than just the Saturday afternoon ballgame.

One thing that she used to say to me as I was growing up was, "Son, if you want something that you've never had, you'll probably need to do something that you've never done." At the time, it really didn't mean as much to me as it should have. In fact, I remember thinking, "Yea mom. What are you talking about? I'm only eight!" But, as I got older I began to understand. If I were already doing whatever it took to get what I want, then, I'd already have it. Wow! Was she smart...or what. Ha! I guess it is true. Our parents do get smarter as we get older.

My point is this. I don't know what it is that you'd personally like to achieve. It could be any number of things like better employees, better customers, better bosses, better profits, more effective use of your time, less stress, or fewer problems. Maybe you've even experienced some of these things in the past and they've simply been lost in the ever-shifting landscape of the workplace. I don't know. But, I do know this. If you were already doing whatever it takes to get it and keep it, then, you'd already have it. So, you're most likely going to need to consider...change. Does that make sense?

Consider this: *Introspection is the most powerful, positive and personal developmental tool that we possess as human beings.* And yet, this tool often goes too long unused. Why?

When I ask this question in workshops some say: "We're just too busy!" or "Things get in the way." What kinds of things? Things like the day, the job, issues, responsibilities, fires, other people, other departments and customers. You know, *things*. Who really has the time to be introspective? No one, and yet here you are reading this little book. There must be something special about you. Congratulations on your commitment to improvement and excellence! Others, when asked about using introspection may say,

"Maybe we're afraid of what we may see." Both of these answers can hold a glimmer of truth, but I think that the bottom line answer is that we just don't think about it. We do what we do because we always have. It is unconscious decision-making, routines or habits that keep us doing the same old thing.

So where do we begin? Most managers have decision-making habits that have been forged in the fire of experience over time. Most of us probably use decision-making habits for two primary reasons. First, these decisions are familiar so we trust them. Secondly, because we are so busy with the responsibilities of our daily activities and jobs we may not perceive the full value in re-thinking or re-evaluating our habitual decisions. Is this a fair assumption?

So why examine them now? Because with the world's changing so quickly and dramatically, many of the decisions, attitudes and approaches that have helped to make us successful in the past may not continue to keep us successful in the future. Consider some of the managers that you've known in the past. Would their management and decision-making style of yesterday be as effective in the business climate and with the employees of today? Many of the tools, attitudes, strategies and techniques of management that have for so many years worked so well, are no longer effective. Why, because the world has changed. The following exercise may provide some illumination.

Exercise:

Read the following statements and ask yourself if you agree or disagree with each statement. Then mark each statement with either *(A)* Agree or *(D)* Disagree.

(A)or(D)

1.) If I take care of the big problems and the little problems will take care of themselves.

2.) New employees should bring responsible behavior to the job.

3.) When I'm busy, staff members should do what I ask of them first and ask questions later.

4.) I'm of value to my people because I've seen and done so much.

5.) Getting results is the purpose of any business team.

6.) Be good to the company and the company will be good to you.

7.) Rule #1: My way or the highway.

8.) Top producers deserve special favors.

9.) I'm an effective manager because I think quickly on my feet.

10.) My job is to support my staff in doing their job.

If you agreed with any of these statements, even though they may have been acceptable and sometimes productive in the past, your decisions may be contributing to issues on the job that limit productivity and hinder developing truly great teams and business relationships. This can ultimately make your job as a manager more difficult. Why? Because change in the workplace necessitates change in the manner we make decisions in order to become more effective.

Please, don't get too worked up. Before you go throw out your whole management tool kit remember, you're already successful! In order to be as successful as you are, you must already know some of the things that we'll discuss in this little book. You may have learned them on your own, often by experience, education or other means. So these things that you have learned have contributed to your success. Still, remember what mother said, if you want something you've never had, you'll probably have to do something that you've never done in order to get it. Or you'll at least need to do something that you're not doing now.

All I ask is that you keep an open mind as you read these pages and uncover these tools and applications. Then ask yourself honestly, "Could this have value for me, my staff, my company and/or my customers. If the answer is yes…well, you know what I'm going to say don't you? Consider changing.

Remember: *Sometimes the most difficult thing to see…is our self, clearly.* Thank you for taking the time and contributing the effort that it takes to keep an open mind. I promise your efforts will have value.

Let's start with a concept that many managers find it easy to be in favor of. Limiting or eliminating re-occurring issues is often a managers' first choice for discussion in a workshop. We'll look at this opportunity in the next chapter as we begin to examine and offer strategies to eliminate the most common decision mistakes.

Chapter Three

Proactive Possibilities

Mistake # 1   Reacting to reoccurring problems or issues in repetitive ways.

You may have heard the statement before, *"Responsibility begins at home."* It's a well-known saying. But what does it really mean? I believe that it suggests that we are all individually responsible, at least to some extent, for the destiny that we produce in our lives. We are first responsible for our own decisions, behavior and results, and then, we are responsible to be the best influence that we can be on others. This could mean that all of the decisions that we make during the day at work are important ones. Before you start screaming, "I can't take this much pressure!" let's talk about decisions.

How many decisions do you make in a day? Do you make more than one? Do you make more than ten decisions? Did you know that the average 16-year-old American makes more than 1400 decisions before 2pm? (Some parents worry that their children can't make a decision. I'm only joking!) Seriously, we're talking about conscious and unconscious decisions that teenagers make starting in the morning when they decide whether they want to get up after the alarm goes off or hit the snooze button.

You have huge responsibility at work, and you're no doubt held accountable for your decisions and the decisions of your staff members by several groups of people which may include your supervisor, employees, customers and other departments. Many of them may hold you responsible for *proactive* decision-making, and yet, you may work in an extremely *reactive* environment.

When I work with service managers, warehouse or installation managers or customer service managers, to name a few, they sometimes say things to me like, "You want to talk about making more proactive decisions? You don't understand what my life is like!" Or they might say, "Why don't you talk to my boss, or the sales department, that's where all my problems come from!" In the same respect many sales managers seem to think that their bosses, their customers, or even their staff prevent them from making more proactive decisions on the job. The truth is, the business environment we work in today is an extremely fast paced, "hurry up and make the decision," or "get the job done no matter what it takes" world. And in all of that, we will be held accountable for our decisions. Welcome to management.

Situation:

Jerry is a sales manager for a local software company. He has had his sales team for about 2 years. At one time it was a pretty solid team, but after loosing a couple of key players 4 months ago, he and his team have continued to fall short of their expected quota. One day, Jerry's boss stops him in the hallway and says, "Are you paying attention?" "How do you expect to make plan if you can't even keep a full team?" Jerry knows that the boss means business. He's seen other sales managers compromise their position because they couldn't make quota with their understaffed team. What should Jerry do?

Decisions:

Jerry decides that in order to regain his boss's confidence he'd better hire someone, and quickly, so he pulls out some old employment applications, makes a few phone calls and hires the first person that walks through the door. (Remember: we're talking about Jerry, not about you.) Now when Jerry meets the boss in the hallway he can say, "Hey boss, I just wanted to let you know that I've taken care of that little problem." The boss says, "Let's hope so." (Do you know anyone who's ever hired in desperation? Don't they usually end up with a desperate situation?)

Complications:

Two months later Jerry's team still isn't making quota. Lucky, his new hire is really happy about having a job because he's been out of work for some time but he's been causing a world of problems with which Jerry now has to deal. Problems like, unhappy customers, dissention among some of his staff members who feel that Lucky is not pulling his weight, interdepartmental issues because he can't seem to get the paper work done correctly, and on top of all of that, the team is still less productive than it should be. Wow! How would you like to be in Jerry's shoes? Who put Jerry in this very troublesome situation? The boss? Lucky? The customers? Was it the other departments?

Consequences:

Jerry's decision to hire Lucky was a reactive one. Reactive decisions often have negative consequences. Reactive decisions have a way of compounding issues or problems. I call this *Negative Leveraging*. Negative Leveraging is a natural outcome to poor decisions. It's a natural compounding of problems that appears to occur with or without our help.

Positive Leveraging takes focus, attention and work. Negative Leveraging can be it's own natural catalyst. Have you ever noticed that?

One example might be this: If you want the plants that you've chosen for your yard to grow well, then you must nurture and care for them giving them the things that they need to grow healthy and strong. Then they'll produce the fruits and flowers that you've anticipated and desired, but have you ever noticed that weeds don't need your help? If you leave a weed alone and don't pay any attention to it at all, it will normally take care of itself and may even choke out the plants that you're attempting to keep healthy. That's Negative Leveraging. Consider the consequences of Jerry's decision. Is it possible that the additional problems that Jerry has to now deal with are the natural, compounded consequences of his reactive hiring decision?

Strategy:

Let's start by distinguishing the true difference between reactive and proactive decisions. Reactive decisions consider primarily the pain of the moment and require that we come up with a solution or decision that will relieve to some extent, that pain. Proactive decisions consider the future consequences that may occur with any decision and require that we make a decision that will create a better future. Proactive decisions are those decisions that keep what in mind? Yes, the future!

It's been well documented that the two greatest motivators for people are *Pain* and *Gain*. Since *Gain* is in many cases a future benefit, which one of these motivators do you think motivates business decisions in challenging situations most often? That's right you guessed it...*Pain*. How does this impact you?

Exercise:

List up to 5 decisions that you've made in the last 6 months at work that may have been motivated by an attempt to relieve the stress, concern, problem or pain that in the longer view didn't turn out as well as you had hoped.

1.) _____

2.) _____

3.) _____

4.) _____

5.) _____

If the next time you encountered one of these issues, you proactively made a different decision is it possible that you might get a better future result? Shouldn't you at least *consider* making a different decision? Many of the managers that I have known say that the answer to that question is yes. Many others have told me that with a closer examination of their difficult situations, they sometimes discover that these issues are recurring problems that stem from habitual reactive decision-making routines.

Making a different decision the next time the situation occurs could relieve the situation or possibly keep it from returning. Shouldn't we at least attempt it? Even if we don't make all of our recurring problems disappear, by making a different decision the next time we face one of these problems we may at least get to experience a new and potentially less difficult consequence!

If asked, Jerry could have no doubt given a number of reasons why it is important to keep a full, well trained and productive team on staff. Why then did he hire so reactively? Maybe he allowed his boss's priority to become his priority. Certainly, having a full crew could help Jerry's team to make quota, but doesn't it need to be filled with the right people? Besides, why should Jerry assume that the boss's priority was simply to fill his team with the next person that he could get to come through the door? Why hadn't Jerry realized that the boss probably wanted him to keep his team full of *high quality* men and women? Maybe the boss really wanted Jerry to be more proactive with an ongoing prospecting and/or recruiting effort to attract and hire the right men and women for his team? Poor Jerry! Do you think that he was more focused on the current *pain* or the future *gain*?

What then can we do to become more proactive? Let's start by putting all of this in the appropriate perspective. I'm not suggesting that you should start second guessing all of your decisions. You are successful men and women, and you got that way because many of the decisions that you make are the appropriate ones for the situation. Trust them.

Still, what about the recurring problems or issues of the day that we face? Have you ever said to yourself, "Even though I know that it's not my job...I'm going to handle this one more time?" Or, have you ever thought to yourself, "How many times am I going to have to tell them...?" At least some of the junk with which we have to deal, we create. We created this junk by making the same reactive decisions in the same reactive situations over and over again.

Is there a difference between reacting and responding? I suggest that there is a difference because they are two different words in the dictionary. The word *respond* suggests that something takes place before we make the decision. What is it that takes place? Yes, Thinking. What if Jerry had taken the time to think more proactively and considered the future gains of effective recruiting and selection instead of focusing on the current pain of the boss's question. Do you think that he would have hired the first person to come through the door? If he had been more proactive might the consequences have been different? Being successful already we shouldn't second-guess all of our decisions, but we should address recurring problems and issues. We've all made decisions in the past that haven't turned out the way we had expected or hoped. Would you like to make a difference in the future?

What if I offered you three simple shortcuts to becoming more proactive? Would you be interested? When I've asked this question in my workshops no one has ever said, "No… I like dealing with all the extra junk!"

If you would like to simplify your life, consider these:

3 Shortcuts to Becoming More Proactive:

1. *Keep a list of recurring problems or issues.*

There's no need to second-guess all of your decisions. You're already successful. That means that you must be making many of the appropriate decisions. But what about the *junk* that just won't go away? As an example, a problem with a staff member that seems to pop up on a regular basis? Or what about the customer issues that always seem to need your attention at the most inconvenient times? Consider the far too often *end of the month push* for your team to achieve your expected levels of productivity. What about recurring interdepartmental issues? Whatever these recurrences are for you…write them down. Why? Because the first step in solving any problem is what? That's right. We must first recognize the problem! By taking the time to write down recurring issues and problems we can then take a little time in the future to think about them and possibly come up with alternative decisions.

2. *When making decisions, attempt to consider the Big Picture.*

Far too often we may allow the *pain* of the moment to outweigh the longer-term *gain* in the larger scheme of things. When you make the next decision to put out a fire, or handle a problem or challenge, you could make the same decisions and take the same actions that you have historically. Or, you could ask yourself, "Does this usually turn out the way I'd like it to, or should I consider making a different decision? What's the *Big Picture?* What are my longer-term goals for this person, this team, this department or this customer?" Sometimes considering the *Big Picture* alters the decision because now the decision-making criteria will be altered.

3. *Look for alternative decisions!*

One of the lessons that I have attempted to teach my children, as I'm sure many of you have, is that no matter how difficult a situation in which we get ourselves; no matter how dark and deep the hole that we dig for ourselves, we can almost always improve the situation in the future. But, in order to do so, we need to consider making different decisions. I'm sure that many of you work in extremely reactive environments. Many of you are required to make quick and decisive judgment calls several times a day. If you have a list of recurring issues and problems you'll find it well worth your time to occasionally take a few minutes to consider this list and the possible outcomes that a different decision in those situations might make? What? You say you don't have any extra time? Well, how much time might you spend now handling the same recurring problem over, and over, and over, and over again? I've learned that you can actually save time in the future if you take the time now to proactively reconsider some of the reactive habitual decisions that you've made in the past! Does that make sense to you too?

Couldn't implementing these 3 simple steps help you to feel more proactively in control in what may be an extremely reactive environment? Couldn't these steps help to relieve some of the repetitive junk that you've had to deal with in the past and present the opportunity to feel a little more hopeful of a more proactive and productive future? Based on the proven implementation of others, yes they can.

Conclusions:

I believe that the majority of the men and women with whom I've had the honor to consult in the past are good people with good hearts. They want to make the best possible decisions in any given situation. Still, it's sometimes difficult when you're deep in the frying pan to know which way to jump. If you're not careful, you may end up in the fire! I recommend a *Re-evaluation Process*.

Once again, I'm not recommending that you second-guess or re-evaluate all of your decisions. You're already successful, but if you're like many managers, you may have some recurring issues. Consider making a different, but more effective management/ leadership decision when you face this situation in the future. Proactive possibilities best present themselves when you:

1. Keep a list of recurring problems or issues.
2. Make decisions while attempting to consider the big picture.
3. Look for alternative decisions!

Exercise: Re-evaluation Process

Refer to your list of up to 5 decisions in the last exercise. Take a few moments to consider the "Big Picture" and possible alternative outcomes. What different decisions might you proactively make in those situations to give you a more desired outcome in the future?

1.) _____

2.) _____

3.) _____

4.) _____

5.) _____

Proactive decision-making is a working style, not an environment. Understanding this allows us to make proactive decisions even in the most reactive environments and situations. It allows us to regain emotional control of our own destiny and future. There are other benefits to this working style. Consistent proactive decision-making is a chosen behavior. Over time, like any behavioral modification, it can have a positive influence on the way you feel about your situation, environment, company and team. Also, consistent proactive decisions on your part almost always guarantees more proactive and thoughtful decisions on the part of your staff who may choose to model your successful management decision making behavior.

By first accepting responsibility for our decisions, and then by working to produce more proactive decisions in the future, we guarantee results that many of the successful men and women I've known were very happy to experience. I believe that you will be too!

Chapter Four

Leveraging Quantum Change

Mistake #2   *Ineffectively managing change in the business or market-place.*

Definitions:

1.) _Leveraging_ To enhance by combining
2.) _Quantum_ Any of the small increments into which forms of Resources and Energy are subdivided
3.) _Change_ To make different

Leveraging Quantum Change   *To enhance a situation by combining resources and energy with the intention of making a difference.*

In 1966 Robert F. Kennedy said as he addressed the nation, "We live in interesting times." I suggest that today we live in extremely interesting and fluidly changing times! I can remember, as you may as well, when the boss could make a decision and stick with it. It wasn't that long ago when being the market leader meant that your company was the largest of the very few choices that customers had in your market place. I was taught that competitive advantage meant that you knew more about your products than your direct competitors. There was a day when customers truly relied on salespeople to provide most of the information that they were going to use to make their purchasing decisions. I can remember job security and product loyalty from customers. Wow! Have things changed!

Consider this, no matter how much things have changed so far; they're going to change even more dramatically and quickly in the future! You might be saying to yourself, "What? It's going to get worse?" It can make you dizzy can't it?

There are two points to keep in mind as we talk about change.

1.) *Change is just an event. How we feel about it gives it power!*
2.) *Change is speeding up!*

Let's review the first point. In his book, "Save Yourself! Six Pathways to Achievement in the Age of Change" Robert D. Gilbreath said, *"Change by itself is neither positive nor negative. It's how we respond to it that determines the outcome."* Do you remember the age-old question, "If a tree falls in the forest, and no one is there to hear it will it make any noise?" Do you know the answer to that question? My answer is, who cares! There's no one there! Change is like that. If change happens across town to someone in some other company, and it has no impact or bearing on you, your family, company, customers, or anyone that you know, and it doesn't have any impact on you, do you really care? Well, do you? Most of the mangers that have come through our workshops have said, "No, not really." Then when *do* we care? Obviously, when it happens to us.

When change happens to us we attach our emotional "price tag". The "price tag" of what this change is going to cost or give whom? That's right, you! You've most likely heard before that we all listen to the same radio station, W.I.I.F.M. *What's In It For Me?* Well, to some extent, that's true. But you know… that's not necessarily a bad thing. It's O.K. to have this built in self-interest mechanism. This mechanism helps us to decide how slowly or quickly we should move when we encounter change. There's nothing wrong with that and, it's sometimes helpful. We simply shouldn't let it control us. The speed at which we adapt to and utilize change should be a conscious decision, and we should attempt to help and influence others to do the same.

What we need to understand is that change is just an *event*. It's simply one of the millions of moments that we're going to experience in life. It has no emotional meaning or value, until we assign one. Once we assign a change event value then... wham! It hits us right where we live! *Change is just an "event." How we feel about it gives it power!* Just remember, a change by itself has no value until we assign it. How you and I, and others choose to feel and what we choose to do when we face change, now that has impact!

Let's review the second point. Change is speeding up! Is that true? Yes it is! If current trends remain the same we're going to experience more change, in technology alone, in the next 3 – 5 years than we've seen in the last 75! "Unbelievable", you say? It may sound so, but I can prove it. Human knowledge, defined as our total understanding of the universe and how everything works, is currently doubling at a rate of about once every 2 years. It took about 5000 years for human knowledge to double the first time. Consider this: 100 years ago the horse was the primary mode of transportation and had been for thousands of years. The world has experienced sweeping changes in transportation in the last hundred years. We've experienced everything from steam engines to space shuttles and the most significant of those changes in the last 50 years.

I can remember when my grandmother said, "Microwaves are evil!" Understandable, since she grew up with wood burning stoves and this was new, unfamiliar technology to her. The microwave oven didn't work on any principles that she understood. It never got hot inside and if you cooked pork in it, the meat would turn gray in color; it must be "evil!" Just imagine what we are going to experience in the next 30 years. How many new advances will we feel are strange?

We must be prepared to leverage all change so that each of us, and our staff can achieve the greatest levels of growth and improvement!

Situation:

Nancy was told in a meeting yesterday afternoon that the job descriptions have just been updated for all of her team members. With the realignment of responsibilities in all departments, (the V.P. had mentioned that "the company needed to trim the fat"), everyone was going to be expected to do more with less. Have you heard that before?

Nancy didn't get much sleep last night because she was expecting a considerable amount of trouble when she introduces this latest and greatest change to her team. She feels that they've experienced an incredible amount change lately, and every time that she's required to offer her team a new change she can almost always expect *push-back* from one or more of her staff. Is it possible that Nancy's expectations of "trouble" and "push-back" might affect the way she delivers the news of the changes to her team?

Decisions:

When Nancy addresses her team in the morning meeting she finally gathers up the nerve to inform them about the changes. With what is clearly a note of hesitation in her voice and pointing to the memo from her boss with the attached new job descriptions in her hand, Nancy begins by saying "Now, you know that *I didn't* have anything to do with this stuff!"

Complications:

As Nancy continues, her worst nightmare begins to come true. It appears as if she's facing a full on employee revolt. A couple of her most valuable players threaten to quit, and one of them, a trusted producer named T.J., an informal leader of the team, actually gets up and walks out of the meeting mumbling something about not taking this kind of stupidity any more.

Nancy obviously made some mistakes. After almost an hour of attempting to get everyone back on track Nancy finally has to come right out and *tell* everyone to get to work; she then leaves the room to track down T.J.

Consequences:

Nancy's not managing the change; the change is managing Nancy. Worse yet, she is literally crippling some of the members on her team to manage change effectively in the future, and is damaging her own integrity along the way through her behavior. Just as importantly, she is driving a very visible wedge between her boss and her. Her behavior is an example of being *unsupportive* to the senior management team and the company. She is also providing the members of her team with the right *not* to support her or any of the changes that she may bring in the future.

Strategy:

Nancy has got some challenges ahead, doesn't she? Allow me to make two brief points. Any manager who believes that they are better off in the face of inevitable change showing a disjointed or un-united management front to their employees is in for a boomerang of extremely negative consequences.

Second, any manager that believes that she can sell 100% of the changes, to 100% of the people, 100% of the time is also in for a rough and bumpy career. And yet, these are relatively common manager mistakes.

So, what's the appropriate approach? It begins with *Support*.

Anytime senior management offers a change then we must support those decisions with the same level of enthusiasm we might have if we had initiated the change ourselves. Even if we don't understand or agree with the initiative at the time that we are informed, we must support it. The true expectation that any company has of all employees is not that they *buy* everything that the boss is selling, but that even if they don't buy it…they'll *support* it. How much better would your life be if every time you offered a change to your staff you knew that you could at the very least count on their support? How much quicker would things actually get done? How many long and arduous employee meetings could be prevented if they would only support? Well, managers are the men and women in the proverbial glass houses. Your employees watch everything that you do and say, and they forget nothing! You could have made a mistake 15 years ago, and if there are any of your old team members still around someone will remember it. So you remember, if you want them to do as you ask, *when it comes to change and support*, ask only as you do. Always support senior management decisions.

Now, let's take a look at which actions should have Nancy taken when leveraging and leading another change? First let's consider a reasonable definition of *Transition Leadership*.

> *Transition Leadership* is the act of influencing others to move forward in the face of change by personal behavior, mentorship and direction.

The following steps for exhibiting *Transition Leadership* would have helped Nancy and could help you with any future transition, initiative or change.

Exercise:

Step One: Define the Transition (What change is taking place?)

Write down a change that you and your team are experiencing, or soon will experience, and list the other departments on which this change may have impact.

Change: _____

Departments: _____ _____

_____ _____

_____ _____

Step Two: Create a list of reasons for the change?

Some managers have told me in workshops, "We can't get all the information and reasons that we'd like to have about some of the changes fast enough. So how do we tell our people what we may not even know?" I think that these students make a good point.

Most everyone finds it easier to make transition decisions if they know *why* something needs to change. Unfortunately, in our world of quantum change, we are sometimes asked to manage a change with requirements to implement with our team long before what many may consider to be a reasonable explanation of *why* is presented to us. Then, as if to compound the issues, normally when the boss asks for something to be accomplished, they want it done when? Many of my students have said, "Yesterday!" So it's important that we understand the *Big Why*.

The *Big Why* is the compelling reason that change, in a growing and thriving business, is inevitable. It also helps us to define and better understand the purpose of any business team. *To serve the customer better, longer and more profitably.* If you don't serve the customer better and longer, someone else will. And, if we don't serve them more profitably we won't have a forum from which to serve them at all. In a fluctuating world and business climate, change is inevitable. Why? Because if we don't stay continually on the lookout for opportunities to change and the opportunities in change we won't be able to best serve the needs of our customers, our company and ourselves.

There are only two kinds of companies in the world. Companies that are changing in an attempt to improve and companies that are dying. What do you think all the mergers, acquisitions, right sizing, down sizing, *out sizing* or what ever it's being called this week, and the *World Economy* are all about? Which company would you rather work for, the company changing or the company dying? That's the *Big Why*.

The *Other Why* is all of the reasons that it's good for you, your people and your company to personally consider this improvement transition. I'm sure that even though it may sometimes be difficult to understand, we should attempt to keep in mind that the *Big Why* and the *Other Why* can be normally, in some ways, connected.

 **Exercise:**

Consider the Change that you wrote down in the last exercise, create a list of reasons for the change. *(Attempt to relate the need for the change to your employees)*

Remember that even if "It's going to be the best thing for the company and customers." sounds like the right thing to say, and that may very well be one of the truths of this transition, that may not be the way all employees prefer to hear it explained.

Reasons:

A.) _____

B.) _____

C.) _____

D.) _____

Exercise:

<u>Step Three: Attempt to keep in mind each employee's personal motivations</u>

Write down each of your team member's names and list at least one reason that it could be important for each employee to "Go Forward" with this transition.
(Remember: W.I.I.F.M *What's In It For Me?* What is important to each of them?)

Team Member Name   **What's in it for the employee?**

_____   _____

_____   _____

_____   _____

_____   _____

Exercise:

<u>Step Four: Develop your proposed implementation plan</u>

Considering the previously determined change, create a list of proposed tasks and completion dates that will help you and your team *Go Forward* with this transition. Then, if needed, create a list of *Resources* and *Relationships* that may be helpful in completing these tasks.

A.) Proposed Tasks and Completion Dates:

_____

_____

_____

_____

_____

_____

B.) Resources Needed:

_____

_____

_____

_____

_____

_____

C.) Helpful Relationships: Ask yourself, "Who are the people *outside* the team who might help improve the effectiveness of this transition? *Examples: other departments, other teams, the boss or peers*

_____

_____

_____

_____

_____

_____

Step 5: Have the meeting with your team

Helpful Meeting Hints:

1.) *Always be honest and open in your communications with your team.* They should always be able to count on your integrity. Even if you don't have all the information that you would prefer to have, if they can count on the truth it helps with their desire to be understanding and cooperative. It's ok not to have all of the answers. If you don't know, say so, and when you do know, share.

2.) *A person's willingness to change is best influenced by Communication and Participation.* Get the individual involved by asking questions and answering questions. This helps the person to feel as if they are better informed and helps the staff member to participate by contribution. Encourage the person to talk. We are all more likely to believe in, buy in and participate in a change when we're the one doing the talking. Aren't you more likely to believe what you think and say than what someone else thinks and says? Remember: You can always tell when a conversation is over...*someone* stops talking!

3.) *Be prepared to answer questions.*
    The people on your team want to know many of the same things that you'd like to know if your roles were reversed. These are some questions that you may consider before your meeting.
    a. Do I understand what is going on?
    b. Do I feel free to talk about it?
    c. How will I be affected?
    d. What are my opportunities/ obstacles?

  e. What are the expectations of me?

  f. Do I have what I need to accomplish this?

4.) *Create a common working Vision*

  a. How will we know when we're making progress?

  b. What "signs" will we see along the way?

  c. How will we know that we've been effective?

5.) *As soon as possible you should attempt to gain Critical Mass.*

This means that you have more influencers moving toward than moving away from the transition. Attempt to gain support of *informal leaders* early in the transition discussions. I'm sure you are already aware that if the informal leaders are with you, everything and everyone will move more quickly. Haven't we talked to our children about this? What's the most powerful pressure in the world? You know the answer... Peer Pressure!

<u>Conclusions:</u>

Anytime you or any of your team is facing a transition remember that *Transition Leadership is the act of influencing others to move forward in the face of change by personal behavior, mentorship and direction.*

Employees today want effective leadership. They especially want and *need* effective management/ leadership in times of change and transition. Remember: *Change is just an event. How we feel gives it power!* Give all the changes you face only positive power and encourage others to do the same. Working *with* change is always more enjoyable and productive than working *against* change. But you already know that...don't you?

Chapter Five

Priority Power

Mistake #3   Making decisions using ineffective or shifting priorities.

The true power in our lives is not produced by what we say; it's produced by what we do! I've learned a few things over the years, thank goodness. One of those things is that if someone is genuinely interested in finding out what is *truly* important to another person, we need not ask them what's important to them; just watch them! Some people may say that their health is important, but they have a hand full of junk food with them all the time and they never get any exercise. Others may say how important their family is, but when they have a day off they seem to always have something more important to do than spend quality time with their children. Some people may say how important their spiritual life is, but their behaviors and pastimes suggests otherwise. Some managers proclaim how important their employees are, but the apparent relationships that they have with their employees are obviously not the healthy, growing, developing, caring, business relationships that they need to be.

Before you decide to very quickly skip this chapter altogether allow me to say this…"Of course we're not talking about *you*! We're talking about those *other* people!" So it's safe for you to read on.

What we're talking about here are people's priorities. Your priorities are those things that are truly important to you. A true priority is your *motivation* to action. When something, anything, is a true priority in life that priority can empower us with all of the strength, vitality and purpose that accomplishment often requires.

My mother, used to ask me, "Why is it that some people that have so much, sometimes accomplish so little, while others that seem to have so little often accomplish so much?" I think I first heard this query when I was about 10. Bless her heart. Based on my experiences, Mom hit the nail on the head again!

Look around. We live in the greatest country in the world! We have opportunities here about which others in the world only dream. One of the primary Freedoms on which this country was founded was freedom of choice. And yet, many people are slow to choose a priority that will actually serve them well in life or in business. What's the answer to Mom's question? The difference between accomplishment and mediocrity is often times a *powerful priority*.

In order to be most purposely successful as manager we need a *powerful priority*.

Situation:

Stephen is a Service Manager for an office equipment company. He's been with the same company for 14 years and he's been a manager for a little over a year. When he was a technician he was literally famous in his company and with his customers as being a *Super Tech*. Stephen never encountered an equipment problem in the field that he couldn't diagnose and make right on the first call. Around the company people have come to call him "SS", short for "Super Steve." Over time, Stephen's team of technicians have learned that if they run into any problem, all they have to do is call "SS" and he'll come running. In fact, Stephen has been known to say, "The team doesn't work for me, I work for the team!"

Stephen received a telephone call at 8:40 this morning from one of his old customers, (now assigned to Ryan), and was told that their machine was down and that the customer's business was in an uproar. Stephen was doing some new hire training with one of his new technicians, but he took the call because the dispatcher said it was an emergency. Stephen knew that the customer was a large company client. He also assumed that Ryan was most likely on his way to his first call of the day and besides, it wouldn't take very long for "SS" to diagnose and repair the problem and then everybody would be happy. So, by 8:47 "SS" was headed out the door, toolbox in hand to help take care of this serious and immediate problem. When asked by his new hire that he had scheduled training with this morning, what he should do while "SS" was gone Stephen replied, "Plug in one of those equipment diagnostic videos, I should be back soon. I'm sorry about this, but you'll learn that in this business the customer always comes first!" Then he speedily disappeared into the mist of the morning!

Decisions:

It looks like Stephen is not short of priorities. It appears that he has a priority to take care of the customers no matter what the cost. It also appears that working for his team, or in this case, doing Ryan's work is a priority. Maintaining his "SS" reputation may be a third priority that Stephen is attempting to serve. If Stephen continues to manage the work and his team this way what will the customers learn? What will his new hires learn? What will Ryan think? And what has his staff most likely already learned?

Complications:

Six months later "SS" is losing his luster. He can't seem to keep his team full of high quality people. He says, "It's hard to find good employees anymore! No one seems to have what he had!" Customer and problem response time has gotten steadily longer on his team, even though a couple of the other teams have shaved their overall response time. Also repair callbacks for his team, because of ineffective diagnoses and repair, are up 21%, and Ryan quit a month ago to work in a completely different industry.

Consequences:

Stephen's true decision-making issue is that he has *priority* problems. He's not lacking for priorities, but his priorities don't appear to serve the real responsibilities or true needs of Stephen's job. Stephen's job is to develop his staff in order to accomplish all goals. I hope for Stephen's sake the V.P. of Service points out *before* he fires him. The long-term consequence of his decisions is that nothing on Stephen's team is really going to get better. As the workload increases, and I'm sure it will in the world in which we work today, Stephen and his staff, along with the company and their customers will most likely suffer. Maybe the next person will do a better job.

Strategy:

Stephen needs a *powerful priority*. He needs a priority that always points him in the appropriate decision-making direction, no matter what the situation, problem or issue. Consider the compass. Which way does the needle normally point? It points north. Does it point toward true north or magnetic north? What's the answer? Who cares! As long as you find your way out of the forest! That's the way our manager priority should work.

When our boss, employees, customers, peers and other departments attempt to pull at you from every angle we need a decision-making priority that always keeps us, and our team moving in the right direction.

What are your manager priorities? What should they be? Maybe I can help you determine what's best for you and your team.

Exercise:

As you examine the motivations to the left and right below, circle one choice that is most important to you from each of the ten examples in either the left or right columns.

Which is most important to you?

	Is this your motivation?	Or	Is this your motivation?
1.	Developing my work skills		Developing my staffs' work skills
2.	Rescuing my staff by handling issues as they occur		Proactively preventing issues from occurring
3.	Personal gratification		Team accomplishment
4.	Working harder than my staff		Working more effectively in less time
5.	Taking more personal responsibility		Delegating to develop my staff
6.	Achieving personal success		Helping others to achieve success
7.	Making all decisions in my department		Empowering my staff to make decisions
8.	Accomplishment under pressure		Less stress and greater results
9.	Trusting myself		Trusting my staff
10.	Getting the job done myself		Developing my staff to get the job done

Now, remember what I mentioned earlier… that if we're genuinely interested in finding out what is *truly* important to another person, don't ask them, watch them.

If someone has been watching you…what would your decisions and behaviors suggest to others is important to you? Does it match what you circled in the "Most Important To You" motivations exercise? The truth is that if you circled anything on the left and you act on those motivations you're most likely sending the wrong message and you're definitely crippling your team's ability to best function and produce the best possible results.

Consider Stephen. Based on his behaviors and decisions, do you think that his motivations would be more on the left of this exercise or on the right? Stephen was definitely on the left!

Think about it; what would your life be like if your staff possessed improved work skills? What if they were developed enough to prevent many of the issues and fires with which you must now personally deal? How much more productive would the team be if each of your staff accepted more personal responsibility for their decisions, actions and results? Would you have fewer fires, fewer employee issues, fewer boss issues, fewer customer issues? And even more importantly, how much more productive would you and your team be? Wow! Just imagine the impact a team like that could have!

In order to build and develop a team like that you need *priority power*. This means that developing this kind of staff and team must become so important to you that every decision that you make leads you and your staff in that direction.

If Stephen had chosen priorities that focused more on helping his staff to achieve success and improve the environment; and focused less on his needs and trying to be "Super Steve" then he would have made different decisions.

First, he would have found some way to satisfy the needs of the customer and develop Ryan's skills and abilities at the same time. This could have been easily accomplished through effective coaching. With the appropriate developmental decisions and coaching Ryan may have handled the problem on his own.

Next, what could Stephen have done differently with the new hire? Maybe he could have had the new hire sit in on his coaching session with Ryan. If Stephen had done that Ryan and the new hire could have both been developing for a more time sensitive positive impact. The new hire would now have more of a feeling of *value* in himself and in his relationship with Stephen and the team. This value is something that I don't believe he got when "SS" threw him into the media center to watch videotapes rather than spend the promised time training him. If nothing else, even if Stephen honestly believed that Ryan couldn't handle the problem, he could have taken the new hire with him and then coached Ryan *on site*. Wouldn't that have satisfied the customer, improved the new hire's perceived value, Ryan's effectiveness, and proven Stephens commitment to each team member's success and possibly provided an opportunity for him to *build up* Ryan in the eyes of the customer? Wow! It's unfortunate that he didn't take full advantage of that opportunity, isn't it?

Exercise: My Priorities

What should your decision and work priorities be? Should they be focused on helping your staff to improve and achieve success? Don't managers really help themselves by helping others?

Create a short list of things that are either now, or you think should be, most important to you in your work as a manager. This list should be focused more on our staff's future gratification and success than on our own immediate gratification and success. (Refer back to the last exercise for inspiration and help if needed.)

1.) _____

2.) _____

3.) _____

4.) _____

5.) _____

Conclusions:

Consider the decisions that you make everyday. What priorities are you serving? Every decision that you make and every action that you take has impact on your team and the inevitable outcomes that will be produced.

Once you begin giving the appropriate amount of focus to decision priorities that help your staff with developing and achieving success, wonderful things start to happen. Your people begin to develop, and many of the employees become happier because they experience a stronger sense of commitment on the your part as their manager. Customers, both internal and external, become more satisfied because you diversify your successful abilities and attitudes *to and through* your staff. John Paul Getty said in an interview with the New York Times, "*I'd rather have 1% of 100 peoples effort than 100% of my own.*" He was right. The true power behind a long term, growing and thriving business has always been being able to duplicate what works with most of, if not all of a company's employees. But it doesn't happen unless you *choose* to make it a priority.

Is there one priority that could envelop and serve all of your other developmental priorities? If you discovered, by going through these exercises, that your priorities revolve around developing your staff to better perform their responsibilities then, allow me to suggest a priority that may help you to *fine tune* your decision-making abilities.

An effective manager's *Powerful Priority* **should be:**

To develop the 4 C's in all of my staff!

What are the *4 C's?* They are:

1. *Commitment* (The commitment to do the right things.)
2. *Confidence* (The confidence in themselves and their team-mates.)
3. *Courage* (The courage to make decisions and face consequences.)
4. *Competence* (The competence to perform their duties well.)

If all of your staff possessed the *4 C's* how much better would everyone's life be? How much better would yours be? How much more effective could your staff become? If Stephen had chosen and used this priority for making his decisions wouldn't the outcomes have been different for him and his team?

 **Exercise:**

In the future, what decisions could you make or actions could you take that might be better for all involved? Create a list of possibilities.

1.) _____

2.) _____

3.) _____

4.) _____

5.) _____

Attempt one or two of these decisions or actions at work and watch the outcomes carefully. I have a strong belief, based on the past experiences of those with whom I've counseled and coached, that you'll be extremely pleased with the short, and long-term benefits of making decisions based on helping others to develop and achieve.

Chapter Six

A.I.M. for Results!

Mistake #4   *Expecting appropriate or effective behavior from staff members without reasonable guidelines.*

Do we need *standards* in the workplace? According to just about anyone when asked that question, the answer will be a resounding "Yes!" But why do we need standards? As explained by a successful manager in one of my workshops, "Without standards you have chaos!" I think that explains the need rather well. Moreover, imagine a workplace where everyone comes to work and only does what *they think* they should do with no understanding or regard for the greater good. Or, when you do attempt to offer direction they sometimes ignore, forget, misunderstand or disagree with the direction that you've given. Are you starting to get a mental picture? You may be thinking, "Wait a minute! I've got a couple of people on my team that do that now." Uh-oh!

Do today's employees want rules? I get mixed answers when I ask this question, but if you talk to employees the answer will most likely be "Yes. But I don't want *stupid* rules." Here's an example of a *stupid* rule. A manager has had a team meeting every Friday morning since the beginning of time. His staff are expected to show up 30 minutes earlier on this day so there will be plenty of time for the meeting before the actual work day begins. If you're late for the Friday meeting there is a hefty penalty to pay and if you miss the meeting, (heaven forbid), you'll get sent home for 3 days and forfeit bonuses for that week. In addition, the manager's meeting is very rarely planned and the employees are convinced that absolutely nothing worth the time and energy that it takes to show up there has ever, or will ever be discussed. These are *stupid* rules!

Situation:

Nakano is having a tough day. John neglected to turn in his activity report for the sixth time this month. Karen and Robert are in an exceptionally foul mood and according to the phone calls that Nakano received from two peer managers, they have attempted to *once again* spread their bad attitudes into other departments. Team productivity is down more than 30%, Nakano had two team members late for work again today and he just received a memo from Human Resources that he can't fire the one person that he had finally made up his mind to get rid of. The memo said something about a lack of documentation. Nakano's wondering "How much worse can it get?"

Decisions:

Nakano decides once again to make a stand. He wonders, "How many times do I have to tell them what to do and how to do it?" "Why don't they grow up?" "Why can't they all just act like professional adults and do what they should do, the way they should do it?" That's what he did when he was in their position. Nakano decides to call a team meeting and lay down the law! In the meeting he tells Karen and Robert that he's received complaints from other managers about their disruptive influence around the company for the last time. He tells John that his reporting process is completely unacceptable, and he had better start turning in his paperwork complete and on time, every time. He says that, "the next person that shows up late for work will pay through the nose." And as his voice reaches a new pitch of irritation, Nakano insists that he's tired of "baby sitting" people that should have learned how to "Act like adults!" by now. Then he grunts an adjournment and heads off to his office. As he walks away, he thinks, "I guess I told them that time!" Told them what? If this has been Nakano's long standing approach to expectation and discipline what do you think that his employees were thinking during his most recent little *do it or else* speech? I wonder how many times they've heard it or something like it before?

__Complications:__

As a result of the latest team meeting two things have happened. First, all of the team members have decided that even if Nakano is having troubles somewhere in his life, he shouldn't come to work and take it out on them! It appears that Nakano's staff members may be having difficulty understanding or accepting their responsibilities. Second, things did get better for a few days. John actually did turn in his reports for nine consecutive days. He was late twice but Nakano figured that it wasn't worth talking about and besides he had too many other "fish to fry." Everything was reasonably quiet in the interdepartmental sector for about a week and then Robert asked someone in payroll "whether she was born stupid or if she had to practice." Productivity went up for six days then dropped by another five percent, and this morning one of Nakano's team called to say that he was going to be late because his alarm didn't go off. "Oh yea...right!" he thought. The late team member happens to be one of Nakano's top producers. Now what is he going to do?

Consequences:

Nakano's decision to "lay down the law" was most likely pointless. You've probably already figured that out, haven't you? The consequences of confrontation without understood, accepted, and consistent standards are often going to be the same. The repetitive outcome can have very little improvement or continuity in employee behavior.

Imagine raising a family without rules, routines, consistent discipline and rewards. What kind of family would you have? Business teams, in many instances, work the same way. Employees want and need rules. But, they want and need rules that make sense to them. *They want rules that are equally applied and consistently enforced.* They also want rules that help them to achieve their goals and desires on the job. By putting good rules in place and keeping them in place, we prove that we care for the people that work for us. If we, as managers, don't provide these logical, reasonable, understandable, and enforceable guidelines, then our staff may begin to feel that we don't really care about them or the team. The consequences can be that we help to create a group of people who don't really care about their teammates or anyone else. I don't believe that this is the final outcome that we're looking for. Do you? The bottom line is that management expectation without true leadership commitment to written standards, coaching and follow-up quite often leads to dissention on the team.

I've learned from working with thousands of successful people that once you learn and apply some fundamental team building techniques building a team is easy. But, keeping a team productive, happy, growing, developing and together… now that's difficult! Consider some of the great teams with which you've been fortunate to be part. How long did the team last? How long did it stay together? And what was the cause of the breakup? According to many team leaders who we've polled, the primary cause for the breakup of a team is dissention. And what is the number one cause of dissention? That's easy; it's *un-adult* like behavior. We're talking about employees that don't do what others think that they should do, or employees that do what others think that they shouldn't. In the opinion of others, these employees might be considered, "trivial, thoughtless, selfish, rude, or un-adult like."

Strategy:

Let's talk about *Standards*. For most purposes, and certainly business purposes, in order for a rule to become a standard it must be six things. Standards must be:

1.) <u>Written</u> (examples include: Job descriptions, memos, etc...)
2.) <u>Easily communicated</u> (common language and terms)
3.) <u>Completely understood</u> (specific, not vague)
4.) <u>Accepted by the staff</u> (supported as a good rule)
5.) <u>Reasonably documented</u> (meets the expectation of Sr. Mgmt, HR, etc...)
6.) <u>Equally applied</u> (no double standards)

Following these simple guidelines in creating a standard proves that *WE CARE* about the team and all of the individual staff members that are part of that team.

Anything else is quite frankly...at best...a suggestion. How much trouble have you seen a manager make for themselves because they were inconsistent with rules and/or discipline? Dissention is a common outcome when *double standards* are applied. How can a manager enforce consistent and positive rules without reasonable documentation? (It isn't pretty is it?) If we care about our staff we must show them by keeping in place any rules making it easier for everyone in the work place to be more productive and happy if they choose to be.

Then what kinds of standards should we consider? Well, that depends on the environment that you wish to create and the outcomes that you wish to produce. So, what do you want to accomplish? One manager told me that she was looking for a "happy medium" with her standards. What is a happy medium? I suppose that's somewhere between a militaristic rules approach and herding cats!

So, what kind of standards should we consider if we hope to gain the greatest possible results from a solidified, productive and lasting team? I recommend that you **A.I.M.** for your required **Results**. Why? Because the true formula for long term individual and team success on the job is:

A+I+M=R

This formula explains the potential of the 4 "Success Standards" categories.

These relationship building and productivity enhancing categories are as follows:

Activities (The appropriate types and number of work related activities)
> *(Added to)*

Interdependence (Attitudes and behaviors which suggest that every employee can perform the responsibilities of their individual job well and chooses to work as a part of an even more productive team)
> *(Added to)*

Momentum (Attitudes and behaviors which suggest that every employee understands and buys-in to the *big picture* and will help one another to reach their fullest business potential)
> *(Equals)*

Results (The more productive outcome that many managers would prefer their collective team to produce)

Let's examine each of the components of this formula individually.

The *Activity Standards* for each employee may be written in job descriptions, rules of engagement, daily activity reporting systems, and performance evaluations. They are most likely written in some format that helps the manager to define, explain, and teach these expected work related activities to each employee. If you find that these activity expectations are not written down and communicated, then it's going to be much more difficult to build the high quality team or reach the greater results that you desire.

The *Interdependence Standards* for each employee may be a little more difficult to find in written format. They are attitudes and behaviors, which suggest that each employee should perform the responsibilities of their individual job efficiently and chooses to work together as an even more productive team. *Interdependence* according to the classical theory (Deutsch, M. *1949- A Theory of Cooperation and Competition*), "positive interdependence encourages team members to *stick together* and transform their diverse inputs into high quality outcomes." According to Deutsch's theory "positive interdependence" means that a person believes that the opportunity for his/ her greatest success is in some way connected to the success of the other members of the team. I've found that the largest challenge for developing and creating *interdependence* within teams is in defining the expected attitudes and behaviors that contribute to it. The productive leveraging of an employee's talents and abilities with others must be taught, coached and developed over time. But first, these attitudes and behaviors must be defined, communicated, taught, and if need be...enforced.

Some possible Interdependence Standards may include:

Interdependence Standards:

1. Accepts personal responsibility for introspection and improvement
2. Looks for opportunity in adversity

3. Perceives other's talents, abilities and opinions as valuable
4. Attempts to understand other's perspectives
5. Attempts to align and leverage abilities with others
6. Complements others openly for good attitudes and behavior
7. Exhibits consistent respect for others

Please keep in mind I'm not attempting to *tell* you what the standards for your team should be. That is of course for you, and possibly your team, to decide. However, I have learned from working with thousands of successful managers that the consequences of not having some or all of these standards in place with the manager and the team can include staff member opposition, dissention, egotistical behavior, resistance to influence, low self esteem, and a general lack of effective productivity by some or all of the staff. So please, at least consider these Interdependence Standards.

Next, let's examine *Momentum Standards*. These are attitudes and behaviors that suggest every employee understands and buys into the *big* team picture, and they will help one another to reach their fullest work potential. *Momentum Standards* can include:

Momentum Standards:

1. Supports company, management and team decisions
2. Promotes frequent and open communication for any possible improvement
3. Helps others to improve
4. Presents all ideas with a *selling* attitude
5. Appreciates the efforts of others
6. Has high expectations for self first and then others
7. Meets or exceeds all company and team standards

Momentum Standards help to keep a team focused on common goals and outcomes that are consistent with leveraging the individual staff members, the team as a whole, the company interest and other departments and resources to a higher level of cooperative and productive achievement. Without these Momentum Standards in place managers sometimes experience dissention, slow or no team and individual improvement, poor interdepartmental communications/ relationships, and less productive results. Hopefully you don't recognize any of these. If you endure them currently or would like to prevent them in the future, please consider *Momentum Standards.*

Result Standards are written expectations that are often supplied by the company for each individual team member. Like activity standards, these are sometimes found written in job descriptions, rules of engagement, daily activity reporting systems, and performance evaluations. You may also find them in individual and team quotas, budgets, and performance goals.

If a manager wants to gain the highest value from all of these standards, then they should use the *WE CARE* approach for implementation. This is the only realistic way to position yourself to positively reinforce your expectations for everyone on the team. This approach has also proven to promote greater levels of *buy-in* for the standards from a higher percentage of the staff members.

Ask yourself, "If my staff was willing to accept full responsibility for all of the tasks, assignments, and activities of their jobs; if they could perform the functions of their individual jobs well and chose to work together as an even more productive team while helping one another to reach their fullest work potential…would my life as a manager be improved?" If the answer you get is "Yes, yes, yes!" Then you're in agreement with many of the students that I've met in my workshops. How do we get staff members to do this? We start by aligning our staffs' daily behaviors and activities with the expected behaviors, or what could become *Standard* behaviors of *Activities, Interdependence, Momentum, and Results.*

Could the 14 Interdependence and Momentum Standards add value to your staff's work environment, relationships, and results produced? Could it make your job as a manager easier? If the answer to either of these questions is "yes", then lets' begin our staff-behavior alignment with a needs assessment exercise.

Exercise: **Behavior Measure-Up?**

Create a list consisting of your name and the names of staff members on your team. Then, considering everyone's previous behavior on the job, compare those behaviors against the 4 *Success Standards* categories to help determine each person's current level of accomplishment for each category.

Name:		Never	Sometimes	Usually	Always
_____	Activities				
	Interdependence				
	Momentum				
	Results				
_____	Activities				
	Interdependence				
	Momentum				
	Results				
_____	Activities				
	Interdependence				
	Momentum				
	Results				
_____	Activities				
	Interdependence				
	Momentum				
	Results				
_____	Activities				
	Interdependence				
	Momentum				
	Results				
_____	Activities				
	Interdependence				
	Momentum				
	Results				

How did everyone "Measure-Up?" Could anyone use a little development?

Conclusions:

Effective Standards are the keys to effective behaviors and results on the job. Of the 4 Success Standard categories, Interdependence behaviors and Momentum behaviors are probably the most difficult for managers to define, implement, and sustain over time. If after reading this chapter, you feel the desire to implement any or all of these Success Standards there are a few effective implementation rules to remember.

1.) **Remember that many of your team members are already successful.** In order to put and keep in place additional, successful standards, you're going to need to help the individual team members understand how this new or consistent behavior will benefit them. (Remember W.I.I.F.M.?)

2.) **Role Modeling is essential.** If you want your people to live inside a particular standard, then who first must live there? You guessed it! It's you! I'm sure that you are presenting the appropriate *role model example* for your staff, but it doesn't hurt to do a little *gut* check once in a while just to make sure that you're doing the right things yourself. As it relates to standards: *Do first, then ask others to do!*

3.) **Implement only standards that you will enforce.** If there is any doubt in your mind that you can't or won't enforce a standard, then don't implement it. Just like with the students in my workshops, I would never suggest anything that might cost your integrity with your team. It would be better for you to have no standards than to attempt to implement something and then not stand behind your convictions. So, be sure that you've chosen standards that you can live with, get behind, and stay behind.

4.) **Implement slowly.** Effective long-term behavior modification is done over time, not over night. Putting your foot down, and expecting immediate and dramatic change, hardly ever works. You didn't get the way you are over night and neither did your staff. We get the way we are over time. Go slowly. Work for buy-in and support from your staff. Be sure footed in every step and then when you're ready…implement.

5.) **Keep senior management informed.** It's always good to let the boss in on what you're doing to grow and develop your team. It's generally far easier to gain support for a plan than it is to explain decisions after the fact. Let senior management know about your plans and then keep them in the loop as your team improves.

6.) **Be optimistically patient.** Remain steadfast in your decisions and have patience. In my experience, as I'm sure in yours, with the right motivations and environment good employees will eventually do the right thing. Show them that you care. Help them understand the value of exhibiting appropriate behaviors. Confront in a *positive* manner all inappropriate or sub-standard behavior. But most of all remain optimistically patient.

I'm sure that like so many others, you'll find over time that the benefits of effective standards far out weigh any challenges that we may encounter in the process of putting them in place and keeping them in place. Just remind yourself, "If all of my staff were willing to accept full responsibility for all of the tasks, assignments and activities of their jobs, if they could perform the functions of their individual jobs efficiently, and chose to work together as part of an even more productive team while helping one another to reach their fullest work potential…would my life as a manager be improved?" And just as importantly, "Would their lives as employees be improved?"

Good luck and good rules!

Chapter Seven

The A.R.T. of Behavioral Improvement

Mistake # 5   Not confronting inappropriate behavior appropriately.

As a manager, how do you feel when you need to confront inappropriate or ineffective behavior? Many have said that it's one of the least favorite parts of their management or leadership roles. Others have suggested that they don't understand why some people just won't "act right!" Some have told me that "it's just part of the job and I'm used to it." The truth is, confronting a staff member's inappropriate behavior can lead to a wide variety of emotions. Most of which, I would venture to guess, are not positive. Have you ever experienced a restless sleep because you knew that the next day you were going to have to confront one of your staff member's behaviors?

If I could offer you a gift, it would be the ability to feel secure in the knowledge that you're making the right decisions, at the right time and for the right reasons when handling employee misbehavior. Dealing with inappropriate or ineffective behavior should be as easy as completing a report, writing a letter, answering the phone, planning for your team, or any of the other processes and tasks that you perform for your job. But, it's not always that easy, is it?

Situation:

Jacob is the manager of a hardware installation team for the local telecommunications company. He's been on the job for 22 years, and he's been a manager for 5 years. He's reasonably sure that he got the job because he was the last person standing and somebody had to do it. He's noticed since he took over the team, the job has sometimes been a little more work than he really expected. Especially when one or more of his staff either neglects to do what they should, or does something that they shouldn't.

He doesn't really mind confronting a person when they are doing something wrong. What he can't understand is why they sometimes keep doing it after he's done talking to them about it. He wonders, "Why aren't they doing the responsible thing?" "He would!"

Today is no different than any other. Greg is late for what has to be the fifth or sixth time this month. Other staff members are occasionally late, but no one is as habitually late as Greg. Greg has worked for the company for 9 years, and it's becoming a company joke that Greg was supposed to be older but...he was born late! He does relatively good work, when he's around to do it, but Jacob sometimes feels that keeping up with Greg and the issues he creates can be a full time job. Jacob has tried to talk to his boss about Greg's habitual tardiness and was told that he should handle the "little" problems himself. "Little problems?" Jacob wonders, how can the boss call this a little problem? Because of Greg's tardiness, Jacob is now having difficulty with some of his other staff members. Every time he attempts to confront their inappropriate behavior they say something like, "Well what about Greg? He's late almost every day, and all I did was turn my work orders in a little late. Why don't you get on his back?"

Jacob knows that he's developing a problem. Things aren't getting done the way that they should. He's developing some disciplinary problems with several staff members. Work effectiveness is down. Customer call-backs are up, and the morale on the team seems to be at an all time low.

Decisions:

Jacob decides to take care of this problem. He decides that if he fires Greg, then everyone else will get the message. He hates to do it. He's been a friend with Greg for years. Their families have been on weekend outings together.

"But what kind of friend takes advantage of a friendship this way," Jacob wonders. "If Greg is going to treat me this way with all that I've done for him and all the slack that I've given him…well then, he deserves what he gets!" Jacob goes to talk to Human Resources

Complications:

Jacob tells Allen, the Human Resources manager that he's going to fire Greg. Allen says that he can't. "What do you mean, I can't?" asks Jacob. Allen informs him that even though he's certainly heard stories of Greg's tardiness, Jacob has never filed any documentation to support his management right to fire. Allen then reminds Jacob of his employee and management handbooks and points out that the appropriate processes for confronting his staff as well as the recommended documentation are all listed there in black and white. Doesn't Jacob remember all the mandatory manager meetings and the discussions of policy and procedure? Apparently, he does not.

Have you ever known someone in Jacob's situation? Is it possible that Jacob feels a little *out of control* in this situation?

Consequences:

Jacob's decision to fire Greg may have been the appropriate one based on Greg's behavior and the negative influences that he was having on the group. But, Jacob's lack of processes in the areas of confrontation and documentation have left him with a no win situation. To make matters worse, somehow the information about his visit to H.R. has gotten back to the team and now the situation is worse than ever. He even heard that Greg called him a "back stabber" to one of the other employees. Poor Jacob. Could all of this have been prevented?

Strategy:

There were a number of decision mistakes made by Jacob. First, he did not have clear and specific guidelines for his staff to follow. If you'll recall we discussed that in *A.I.M. for Results*. Second, Jacob didn't seem to have any repeatable, consistent process for confronting inappropriate or ineffective behavior. This is proven by the fact that his staff not only continued inappropriate behavior but it had gotten steadily worse. Last, Jacob didn't follow the appropriate guidelines given to him by the company and H.R. How does he expect to get support from the boss or Human Resources when he doesn't document his confrontations so that everyone is aware of the severity of a problem?

For our purposes, let's resolve the second issue. I'm not suggesting that the first issue isn't just as important, but we addressed that issue in *AIM for Results* so let's assume that there are already *WE CARE* standards in place in Jacob's company and/or on his team. Jacob's lack of repeatable, consistent processes for confrontation is no doubt the bones of his problem. I believe, and so do most of the successful men and women with whom I've had contact over the years, that there should be a consistently reliable process for confronting inappropriate behavior for all staff members.

There should also be different levels of confrontation for different levels of inappropriate behavior.

These levels are the *A.R.T.* of behavioral improvement.

The *"A"* represents the approach style for the minor infractions committed by a staff member. As an example, perhaps a staff member shows up late for work one time in 3 years. If you have a standard in place that states everyone is required to be on time and a staff member shows up late, then confronting the behavior is a necessity, but it's still a minor infraction. The approach style is to *Ask* by way of *casual conversation* why the infraction has occurred. In this way we confront the minor infraction with a casual, positive, and non-confrontational approach.

The *"R"* represents the approach style for an infraction that is more severe than for a minor infraction. As an example, perhaps a staff member acts immature with another staff member, e.g....bickering or intimidating. The approach style is to *Reason* with the employee. We want to offer him a *constructive critique*, to help him to understand why this behavior is in conflict with the team or company's standards. Often times this can be accomplished by simply asking the staff member how this particular behavior is in conflict with established and respected standards.

The third approach is the *"T"* which stands for *Transfer.* In these most severe situations we should to transfer responsibility or ownership for their actions to the staff member. Then, we should require a *compelling commitment* on the staff member's part to change his behavior and if needed help him to create a reasonable improvement action plan. Once again, this approach is reserved for the most severe infractions of inappropriate behavior.

The 3 levels of constructive confrontation are:
A –Ask (Casual Conversation)
R –Reason (Constructive Critique)
T –Transfer (Compelling Commitment)

The purpose of the 3 levels and corresponding approach style is quite simple. If someone commits a minor infraction of inappropriate behavior, then later commits a different and more serious offense, they should be approached in a way that is warranted by the seriousness of the offense. In that way, they very quickly understand the severity of the mistake and will be encouraged to more quickly understand the severity of the consequences for everyone involved. This helps people to more readily accept responsibility for their actions and motivates them to change their behavior.

Isn't that why manager confront staff members in the first place? Don't we confront our staff because we want them to change their behavior?

Let's examine these three approaches more closely. In all three of these constructive confrontation correction strategies we must not loose sight of our ultimate objective, to motivate the person to change his/ her behavior. The tone of your approach is very important. I don't just mean the tone of your voice. I mean the tone of your intentions and delivery as well. A great manager must take on many roles with their staff. Accepting responsibility for your staff member's behavior and constructively confronting the inappropriate or ineffective behaviors is one of those roles, but it should be done in a respectful, professional, and positive manner. It should be done in the way that you would like to be treated.

The first approach is for the minor infraction.

Level One: *Ask* (Casual Conversation)

Example: (A staff member shows up late for work one time in 3 years.)

Karen, I've never known you to be late. Are you O.K.?

This *Ask* approach doesn't assume that the person has intentionally broken the rules. There may be a situation or problem that impaired the staff member's ability to do what they normally do which, in this case, is to show up for work on time. It also shows concern for the individual, not just for the rules and standards. This is extremely important.

Level Two: *Reason* (Constructive Critique)

Example: (A staff member harshly criticizes and demeans another employee)

> *Rick, based on the standards that we have for everyone that works here, how should you have handled that situation?*

This *Reason* approach assumes that the staff member knows, and usually follows, the same standards and guidelines that the rest of the team follows. Often, by offering the staff member time, opportunity, and a reasonable constructive confrontation process they need very little input from someone else in order to initiate behavioral improvements.

Level Three: *Transfer* (Compelling Commitment)

Example: (A staff member falsifies a document)

> *Dave, in your opinion, why was your behavior inappropriate; and how can we insure that this doesn't happen in the future?*

This *Transfer* approach assumes that the staff member has or will accept responsibility for his/her actions and is willing to take all necessary steps toward improvement. This doesn't mean that the staff member will know or even offer a complete *repair* for the problem or situation, so you may need to brainstorm with him to come up with a realistic and responsible approach for future improvement. Also, don't forget timelines for actions or improvement. With the more serious offenses, action plans need timelines. There is no action in an action plan without a timeframe. Help the staff member to make the corrections in a timely fashion, and follow up with them to insure that they have done as they committed to do.

Do these approaches make sense? If you give them reasonable consideration I'm sure that they will. In fact, you may already be doing something similar to this on the job already. Offering levels of positive and constructive confrontation to different levels of inappropriate behavior isn't a new concept. It has no doubt been around as long as parents have been raising children.

Ask yourself this question, "When I was a child, how did I know when I was in real trouble with one or both of my parents?" Didn't they sometimes do or say something differently depending on the severity of the offense? Some people have mentioned that their parents used their full name, or called them by their given name, instead of their nickname. Others have told me that their mother might say, "You wait until your father hears about this." Whatever the parental behavior, many parents had different strategies they used to approach different levels of inappropriate behavior. This approach let us know when we needed to accept more responsibility or take more care in the future.

If you would like to use this *ART*-full approach or simply enhance your already successful constructive confrontation styles there are two things to consider.

First, which inappropriate behaviors should receive which approach?

Exercise:

Consider the standards that are currently in place with your company and/or your team. In which level of infraction do they belong? (Minor, Medium or Severe) Once you've made that determination, list the appropriate constructive confrontation level for each listed infraction. *Remember, we shouldn't confront without the WE CARE standards.*

Broken Standard	Infraction Level	Confrontation Level
(WE CARE)	(Minor, Medium, Severe)	(Ask, Reason, Transfer)

1. _____   _____   _____

2. _____   _____   _____

3. _____   _____   _____

4. _____   _____   _____

5. _____   _____   _____

6. _____   _____   _____

7. _____   _____   _____

8. _____   _____   _____

If you have more than eight standards with which to work then attempt to prioritize the most important standards and start with those. This common sense process of listing and categorizing infractions and confrontation approaches will help you to be more consistent with your approach with staff members in the future. Your consistency will also send the message that you care *equally* about all of your staff members. Isn't that a great message to send?

Second, lets address the need for support in your decisions and constructive confrontations from other levels of management and possibly other departments. e.g. Human Resources

Exercise:

What paperwork and procedural expectations are already in place in your company as it relates to coaching, confrontation and firing? On a separate sheet of paper make a written explanation of your understanding of these paperwork and procedure expectations.

Once this exercise is completed, take your written understanding to the appropriate managers or departments and clarify their understanding with yours. It's usually wise to attempt to be on the same page with your boss or Human Resources.

Conclusions:

Staff members today want rules, but they want and deserve *WE CARE* rules.

We discussed this in *AIM for Results. WE CARE* is the acronym for *W*ritten, *E*asily communicated, *C*ompletely understood, *A*ccepted by the staff, *R*easonably documented, and *E*qually applied. What you and I have approached here are the strategies that allow you to communicate, document and apply the team and company standards in a way that is most easily accepted by the majority of professional adults on the job today.

By creating a repeatable process for positive, consistent and constructive confrontation you'll spend less time handling inappropriate or ineffective behavior because staff members will learn from their mistakes more quickly and be more likely to accept a higher degree of responsibility for their actions. Isn't that what we really want? And, by aligning your decisions, procedures and documentation with the company policies and procedures you will proactively eliminate issues and challenges with the boss and other departments in the future.

As pointed out by one of the professionals who I met at one of my workshops, "This just seems like common sense to me!"

Chapter Eight

The Performance Highway

Mistake #6   Making Decisions without Vision.

A wise man that I knew once said, *"When you don't know where you're going...all roads lead there!"* Think about it. If we work through the day with no specific, consistent destination in mind and no on-going, written plan to guide us, how could we ever really know for sure when we've arrived? I believe that without the appropriate guiding direction a plan can provide, our decisions tend to offer us, and our team, less time on the *Performance Highway* and more time floundering on the roadside.

As I have mentioned once or twice before in this little book, you're already successful. I don't believe that any of the thousands of people that I've met in any workshop attended, or were sent there, because it was some valiant last effort to save their career. Just like you, they were already successful. What I'm suggesting is this, often times a manager's current decision success can be based on their previous experiences. These experiences can be woven into their successful management style.

One example of this is when our experience allows us to erect *guardrails* along the performance highway to occasionally keep us from running completely off of the road. Managers learn over time that there are certain decisions that will serve them better than other decisions in a given situation. These are the *guardrails*. The fact is, that these guardrails are constantly being tested, challenged, and sometimes even removed by other people and the priorities that they have for your staff members, your decisions, and your time. Bosses, employees, customers and other departments may attempt to build off ramps that can detour us from our most productive, successful, and happy route with our team. Have you ever experienced this?

What's your life like when you get pulled off of the *performance highway* too often during a day? Do you sometimes go home feeling less fulfilled, less satisfied and less content with your day than you would like? Do you sometimes feel like there just isn't enough time to get everything done? I would love to see every manager go home at the end of the day feeling completely satisfied and confident that they fulfilled their responsibilities to the best of their ability and that they made the right decisions, at the right time, and for the right reasons. Would that help some of us to rest and sleep better? Would that allow some of us to leave the work day behind at the appropriate time and focus a little more on the people that love and support us at home. Why do some managers drag home their work day and then dump it out on the dinner table at night with their families?

Years ago, when I had one of my first management positions, I took two of my children to a Saturday matinee for a promised "day out with dad." The movie was one that they had been looking forward to seeing for some time, and even though I had a million other things to do, I knew that the promise had been made and should be kept. So off to the movie we went. After the movie, we were on our way to get pizza when my son said to me, "Dad, did you like that movie?" I said, "Sure, did you?" Then he said, "Oh yea! Hey dad, what was your favorite part?" At that moment it occurred to me that I had just sat through a two-hour movie with two of the people that I cared most about in the world and hadn't even seen the movie or experienced their enjoyment of it. How sad is that? Guess what I had spent that two plus hours thinking about? You guessed it! Work! I didn't want my children to know how rude I had been, so I quickly responded with, "Wow! I thought the whole movie was good! What part did you like best?"

That got me off the hook that time, but I decided that things needed to change. I needed a written plan that would allow me to leave work each day knowing that I had accomplished the appropriate tasks of my job and met the responsibilities which I needed to so that I could go home with a clear conscious allowing me to focus on the other priorities of my life. How about you?

Situation:

Michael is a Managing Partner in his document reproduction firm. His branch has been financially successful over the last couple of years since he took over. He's helped the business grow by 13% in the last year and personally made more money than ever, but Michael has no real life outside of work. He puts in 14 – 16 hour days. He normally works 6, and sometimes 7, days a week. He is on constant pager and cell phone alert with customers as well as employees. He hasn't had more than a 3-day working vacation in 3 years, and he is always hiring and training new employees due to the employee burn out factor that seems to exist in his business. To keep a working staff of 14 outside sales associates and 26 full time production people, he's hired and trained 22 people in the last year alone. Michael receives corporate objectives for productivity and profitability every quarter. It has been somewhat difficult, and yet he's done a good job of keeping up with corporate expectations, plans, and projections so far. Still, other than a lot of hard work and long hours on his part, he's not really sure what has taken him and his team to their previous levels of success. His standing rule for himself and his team is, "Get the job done…whatever it takes!"

I wonder how many managers plan and lead their teams to success, and how many managers just work very hard and happen to routinely achieve success at the end of the month? The latter is what Michael did and it's worked for him…up to now.

Decisions:

Michael received his team's quarterly projections review this morning from corporate headquarters and his projection has been increased by 14%. When he called his boss for an explanation of the new projection, he was told that according to market assessments, Michael's local market has grown by 63% in the last year and he's not taking full advantage of the opportunity. Michael decides to have a meeting with his sales team where he intends to focus on daily activity successes and failures. He has determined, before the meeting, that all of his people will simply need to work harder and make more calls if they are going to help him meet this new projection. He knows that some of his sales associates need more development, and this may put added pressure on their daily performance but with the larger expectation to achieve this quarter, he decides that he won't have time for anything except direct selling support. You know, closing deals, putting out fires, pushing paperwork. So, they need to find a way to "take up the slack" and be responsible for their own improvement.

Complications:

By the end of the following month Michael has bigger problems. It's becomes obvious that he's not going to hit his monthly business plan objectives. In fact, he's actually going to be short of his original expectations. Part of the problem is that he's had 3 sales associates leave the company in the last 25 days. Two of them told him that his expectations for daily sales activity were just "way out of line." The third said that, "I just can't do this job." Michael is spending more time at work now than ever, and he didn't think that it was even possible to do so. His boss is definitely going to want to know why the "number" isn't coming in this month and what Michael intends to do about it. And to top it all off, he's in the "dog house" with his family because he missed his daughter's birthday party when he got hung up with a customer complaint last week. (Does anyone out there want to trade places with Michael?)

Consequences:

Things change in business continually. Have you noticed that? It appears that the only constant in the universe is change itself. When Michael received his newly increased expectations from corporate head-quarters, why didn't he refer to his written, ongoing team and individual developmental plans to find out what decisions should be made to improve productivity in order to meet the changing demands. Could it be because he didn't have a written developmental plan? (I'll bet that he wished that he had one now.)

The consequence of making *Decisions without Vision* is that we some-times make decisions that lead us to the wrong destination, or to a place where there is no road at all! We talked briefly about the importance of considering the *Big Picture* in *Proactive Possibilities.* How can anyone make consistent, effective decisions without keeping the big picture in mind? How can we be proactive and avoid the hazards of business without some *map* of plans and destinations that will lead us, and our team to our desired results. This suggests that we not only need a written *business development plan*, but that we also need a *people development plan* that works cohesively with and compliments company plans and objectives.

Do you have any employees who are sometimes having difficulty seeing their future inside your company? Michael did! Do you sometimes have difficulty achieving the results that the company expects from your team? Michael did! Do you sometimes work very hard only to fall short of the expectations that you and the people you care about would like you to achieve? Michael did! These consequences are often the direct result of no written individual/ team development plan. You're no doubt successful. Maybe if you don't have these written plans, you could go right on being successful. Maybe you could, but what if things change? Could remaining successful be more difficult than it need be?

Strategy:

Senior management often offers business plans and written expectations to managers and their teams. Certainly we should pay close attention to the boss's expectations and do whatever is in our power to achieve them. A team growth and developmental plan is one way to support that effort, but there are other reasons that a written developmental plan is important.

Why are you successful? Statistically, very few managers have a written personal and/ or team development plan. If you are a manager who hasn't used written developmental plans to achieve consistent success, then how did you become so successful? One manager's answer to that question was, "The cream always rises to the top!" Maybe that explains the outcome, but in my mind it doesn't suggest the reason that many managers are somewhat successful without a written plan. The answer, I've found, is quite simple. I've found that unplanned but successful people seem to have certain things in common.

These managers seem to be able to create a clear picture in their mind of what they want to accomplish. At least a clearer picture than the majority of people are capable of envisioning. They also seem to be driven by some desire to accomplish this vision by holding onto the picture longer than most people appear to be capable, and because of that are then motivated to work harder to achieve it. Lastly, most of them seem to possess the raw power or tenacity that it takes to stick with the job and continue to work harder until they achieve at least some of what they envisioned. This is the simplified reason for many managers' success. Does any of this sound familiar? According to many of the successful people without written plans with whom I speak, it does.

I have a question. Even if you possess these special abilities that some other successful people also possess, do all of your staff have these same abilities? I've discovered from talking to numerous managers and employees that the answer is, no. In fact, quite frequently these days, we find that more and more employees are having difficulty seeing any future, especially theirs, inside their current company. So what can we learn from this? We can learn that another reason for having a written, individual and team development plan is that you can use it to help tie the daily development and activities of your staff to some longer-term future that they would like to see achieved inside their current role or position with your company. With more hope for the future…comes longer tenure!

Longer vision from employees translates into more focused work, better work, less attention to the short-term adversities that they may face and longer tenure from high quality employees. Employees today want *Leadership*. Great leadership helps them to focus on the *big picture*. Written plans helps us, and them, stay focused on what's truly important. If we can do that, our decisions, and theirs, based on those plans, allow us to accomplish goals that together we set for the team.

Just as importantly, when we start to get caught up in the *fray of the day*, when the priorities of others require that we make decisions, our written plans create additional *guardrails* on the *Performance Highway* to keep us, and our team, on the right track.

Besides, if we don't work with specific, written team development plans, and if we don't require that our staff members continually work toward improvement, might we at some point find ourselves in Michael's situation? It may happen that we could find ourselves needing to meet greater expectations and not have the high quality people, tools, or abilities to achieve them? What will be the expectations on you and your team in the next year? Do you think that the expectations will be greater, or less, than they were this year? What has been expected historically?

Improvement? We all know the answer to these questions. If we're going to stay in business, we must always seek improvement.

So where do we start? We must start by catching the "Vision!"

(Step One: Catching the Vision)

 **Exercise:**

In the space below answer this question.

If I had unlimited time, resources, and support from my company as well as all of the right people, what would my team become?

Remember: This is a vision. A vision is more like a dream than a reality. This vision should be long range and possibly help to define any mission that you may have for your team. Dare to dream!

(Example: My team will be the most proficient, profitable, and best respected team in the company!)

_____

_____

_____

_____

_____

(Step Two: Clarify Objectives)

Objectives are *Goals* to be accomplished or *Problems* that need to be solved in order to achieve your longer term Vision. Why *Goals* or *Problems*? That's easy. Some of us see ourselves as *Goal Setters*. Others of us see ourselves as *Problem Solvers*. Which way do you see yourself? Either way, the outcomes can be just as powerful if you consider using a common planning process for achievement.

You've probably heard somewhere before that in order to correctly and most effectively identify a goal or a problem it should be *S.M.A.R.T.E.* This process for identifying goals or problems is not new but still extremely important. What does *S.M.A.R.T.E.* mean?

Specific
Measurable   (Specific + Measurable = Quantifiable…Improvement can be calculated.)
Attainable
Realistic   (Attainable + Realistic = Improvement should be realistically attainable but a goal that you and possibly others must work to achieve. A stretch goal.)
Timely   (Time Lines. There is no action in a plan without timeframes.)
Emotional   (You must be emotionally committed. It must be something that you want and believe is important. *Passion tenders the fire of action!*)

Exercise:

Create a beginning list of goals or problems that need accomplishment or solutions which might help to achieve your team vision. Your beginning list is just that, *a beginning list.*

It is not necessary that you come up with everything that has to be done in order to accomplish your vision. It is only necessary that you begin. Things change. People change. Company goals change, and so might your goals.

Three rules for creating goals or determining needed solutions:

1.) *Be flexible with yourself.* Remember that any real improvement with your staff is generally well received, whether you achieve your beginning vision or one that is created later with your team as they improve or things change. So be flexible with yourself. Allow yourself, your team, and your goals to change as the things around you change.

2.) *Take small steps.* Neither you nor your staff members got the way they are *over night.* They got the way they are *over time.* Rome wasn't built in a day and neither will a great team. Besides, you probably have plenty to do already, even without your new plan. Putting huge pressure on yourself to accomplish new things when you're currently short on time during the day will encourage you to stop working your plan. That wouldn't be good for anyone involved. So, take small steps.

3.) *Work in areas of Control or Influence.* There's no point in writing down things that you can't currently do. Do the best you can to come up with goals or problems that you can control or influence in some positive way.

What *Goals* should be accomplished or *Problems* should be solved in order to achieve my vision for the team?

(Goal example: I will have a full, initially trained, completely competent team by November 31st of this year!)

Goals/ Problems: **Dates:**

1.) _____   _____

_____

_____

2.) _____   _____

_____

_____

3.) _____   _____

_____

_____

4.) _____   _____

_____

_____

(Step Three: Pitfall Prevention)

Exercise:

What *hazards* or *pitfalls* may I foresee in attempting to accomplish my plans? What are my plans to avoid these *pitfalls?*

You may not envision any pitfalls on your way to achievement, but sometimes challenges do get in the way. If any possible pitfalls come to mind as you create your plans, I recommend that you write them down. If they do present themselves along the way, you'll be better prepared if you've proactively considered the pitfalls and plans to avoid them. Maybe you could eliminate, alleviate, or prepare for the situation before it becomes a pitfall?

Pitfalls: **Plans to Avoid Pitfalls:**

1.) _____   _____

                                           _____

                                           _____

2.) _____   _____

                                           _____

                                           _____

3.) _____ _____

_____

_____

4.) _____ _____

_____

_____

(Step Four: Solicit Help)

Exercise:

Who could help me achieve my plans?

There is nothing wrong with accomplishing your plans with the solicited help of others. In fact, other people and their experience, opinions and knowledge can sometimes speed up the achievement and success curve for you and your team. Some of your staff may also be of help. What about the boss? Other managers? Consider who might have the ability and willingness to help you.

Name/ Department/ Company

1.) _____

2.) _____

3.) _____

4.) _____

__Conclusions:__

There are reasons that planning is important to you and your staff on the job. We've discussed some of them. There are also reasons that planning works to help us make better and more proactive decisions. We've also discussed some of those.

What we haven't discussed is why planning makes successful people even more successful. The interesting truth is, that there is a Law of Nature that governs success. I call it the *Law of Acquisition.*

Law of Acquisition "Anything that you think about long enough and hard enough is bound to come true."

I believe that this is a gift that we have all been given, and I've learned that we use it whether we realize it or not. What we think about and upon which we focus our effort is what we acquire in our lives. If you focus on bad, you acquire bad. If you focus on good, you acquire good. And if you focus on nothing, well…you acquire nothing. (That may not be completely true. You may acquire a surprise!) According to James Allen, a 19th century Englishman, in his book *"As a Man Thinketh"*, "All that a man achieves and all that he fails to achieve is the direct result of his own thoughts." I've found this to be true. But what happens to a manager and the team if the manager doesn't focus on positive development for himself/ herself and the team? Just as focus produces results; the lack of focus produces the opposite. Does that make sense? What happens if a manager chooses to neglect written, positive developmental plans? Nothing! And I mean nothing! At least nothing consistently good happens. People do what they've always done, and they get what we've always gotten. Of course as the world, people, and business continually changes around us, it can become more and more difficult to keep up with the high performance demands because we spend less and less time on the *Performance Highway* and more time in the *ditch*. Wasn't that true with Michael?

So the answer is to continually focus on writing and improving written developmental plans for yourself and your team. These plans should be written, focused on team development and improvement, be in concert with company plans, have specific tasks to be accomplished, and should be reviewed and/or changed on a regular basis. Remember what the man said, "When you don't know where you're going...all roads lead there!"

Do you have a plan?

Chapter Nine

Improvement Coaching

Mistake #7 *Expecting reasonable staff member improvement without effective coaching.*

I remember hearing once that "The best way to predict the future is to create it!"

What kind of future are you predicting for yourself and the individual staff members that make up your team? We've discussed several things that might help us to predict a more powerful and positive future. Things like being more proactive, effectively managing change, prioritizing development and decisions, setting and implementing positive standards, and planning. Still, even with these and other visionary and developmental processes in your management arsenal you still could fall short of developing your team to it's fullest potential. If you don't offer consistent, effective, and ongoing coaching at the right times to those who are in need, there is no way to effectively predict a positive outcome. *Success is a road always under construction*. If planning is the vision and blueprint to our future, effective improvement coaching is the solidified stairway that carries our staff members and us to that brighter and more productive existence.

<u>Situation:</u>

Susan manages a lender funding team. Her team's responsibility is to verify applicant information referred to their office and make sure that the application *holes* are filled, and that *no rock is left unturned* by verification. Obviously, the company allows very little room for mistakes in this process for Susan's department. She currently has twelve staff members on her team. Three employees were hired within the last nine months. Four of her staff members have been with the company between one and two years, and the rest have been with the company for two or more years.

Susan has a number of challenges with her team, but what really concerns her most is that she often feels that staff members are making slow, or no improvement in their ability to do their jobs or in contributing to the cohesiveness, effectiveness, and improvement of the team.

The company has in place requirements for *workload* and *volume* improvements that are expected of every member of her team. And yet, because many of her staff are not making personal improvement quickly enough, she spends many hours cleaning up details that most of her staff should be able to handle on their own by now long after everyone else has gone home. Susan sometimes wonders, "Why don't they care?" Or, "How many times am I going to have to tell them…?"

Mark, who's been with her about five months, seems to make more than his share of mistakes every day. Ron, who has been a team member for about eight months seems to have a problem with motivation and complains more than any two people that she's ever met. And Carolyn, an employee of the company for more than seven years, seems to enjoy telling others what they're doing wrong rather than doing her own job, and based on her tenure, she should be much more effective than she is at present.

Some of Susan's staff members have made some improvements in their performance, but nothing measurably consistent since Susan took over as department manager three years ago.

Decisions:

Susan decides to share with the team the company expectations of their productivity and effectiveness based on their tenure. She's done it before, but decides that she'll try it "one more time." During the meeting, she pulls out the "workload" and "volume" guidelines created by the company. She then does comparisons with each employee to point out where they each could use improvement. She also recounts the long hours she spent last month cleaning up after them and filling in the *holes* that they had left in their work. She then tries to end the meeting on a positive note by saying that she believes in each of them and that she knows that they all possess the abilities to do better work. Her final comment is "Now dig down deep and let's make it happen!"

Complications:

Over time it appears that Mark and his mistakes are getting worse. Susan wonders, "How many times does he have to be told before he gets it?" She has begun referring to Mark in private as "the one with little learning problems."

Ron can't seem to put two good attitude days together, and other members of Susan's team have asked her to move him into an area of the office by himself because he attempts to talk to everyone about his *issues*. It is becoming more difficult for them to get their work done.

Carolyn's productivity has dropped almost completely off the chart since the two employees that had more tenure than she have quit. One of the two employees that left said that they were "unhappy with the work environment" and felt it had gotten to be a real "bummer" to even show up for work every day. Carolyn seems to agree with the "bummer" statement, but she keeps showing up for work. Have you ever experienced a tenured employee who you know is capable but isn't reaching toward their greater working potential? I've been told, "The only thing worse than an employee that quits and leaves, is an employee that quits and stays!"

What could help Carolyn and Ron want to make attitude and work behavior improvements? What could help Mark dramatically improve his work effectiveness?

Consequences:

The consequences of Susan's decisions can be significant. Whenever a manager leaves improvement or development solely to the individual that needs it, the improvement will most likely be slow in coming, if it happens at all. No matter how well defined the guidelines and expectations, we all need effective coaching from time to time to help us learn and develop more effectively and rapidly.

What if your parents had said, "This is life...this is what we expect...figure it out." Would maturing have been a little more difficult for you? I'm not suggesting that we need to give every staff member daily tutelage; however, we must be prepared to offer effective coaching in a style that will be best received, most helpful, and influential to our staff when they need it if we expect them to make improvements effectively and quickly.

If we don't provide adequate coaching, then the little to no improvements can be the consequence in addition to a poor work environment, boredom with their jobs, disgruntled employees, staff members feeling that no one really cares, and a lack of enthusiasm or respect for the job, the company and you. All of these may lead to the inevitable outcome of poor behavior, poor production, more turnover, and greater time and effort requirements for the manager of the team. Who really wants that? Not any of the successful men and women whom I've met over the years!

<u>Strategy:</u>

Develop an ongoing coaching process that offers what your staff members need when they need it.

Let's start by recognizing that effective coaching is a process that can be molded to best fit the individual based on their current improvement needs, competency levels, and willingness to be coached. Coaching should be a process of partnering with the staff member to enhance communication, cooperation, and improvement. It should involve high levels of active participation by the staff member in order to create higher levels of buy-in for new attitudes, strategies, and behaviors that are often required when making any improvement of performance or effectiveness.

This coaching model is called *The Partnering Process* and is made up of four basic improvement components subdivided into 8 coaching steps.

These components and steps are:
1. *Evaluate* (Observe and Identify Need)
2. *Discover* (Uncover Causes and Determine Objectives)
3. *Plan* (Weigh Alternatives and Develop Actions)
4. *Implement* (Align Resources and Initiate Action)

The Partnering Process

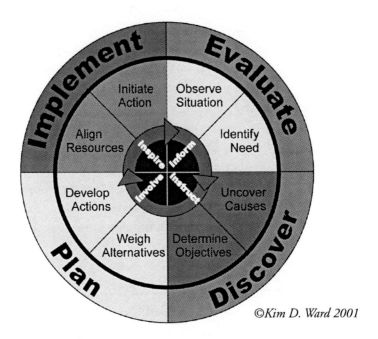

©Kim D. Ward 2001

Different staff members need different levels of assistance in each of these improvement steps depending upon their tenure, experience, aptitude, attitude, the current situation, and numerous other variables. To best serve our purposes, let's narrow the variables down to two primary focus areas.

These two developmental focus areas are:

1. *Competency* (A persons ability to perform the tasks of their job)

2. *Willingness* (A persons desire to perform the tasks and be coached for improvement)

Understanding a staff member's levels of *Competency* and *Willingness* help us to determine which coaching approach should be used in order to most quickly and effectively help the person make improvement.

There are 4 coaching approaches in the inner circle of development in our coaching model. One or more of these approaches are applied based on the current level of *Competence* and/or *Willingness* of the individual staff member:

A. **Inform** (*Competency*-yes, *Willingness*-yes)

B. **Instruct** (*Competency*-no, *Willingness*-Yes)

C. **Inspire** (*Competency*-yes, *Willingness*-no)

D. **Involve** (*Competency*-no, *Willingness*-no)

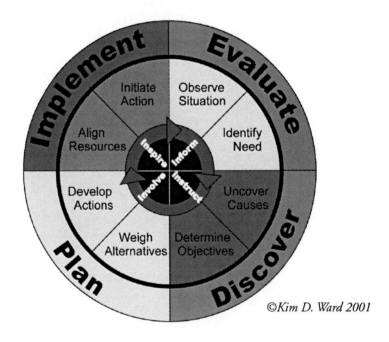

©*Kim D. Ward 2001*

Each of these coaching approaches requires different levels of communication, information, participation and facilitation on the part of the manager.

Exercise:

Create a list of your staff members. In your opinion, the last time that they needed coaching or developmental help from you as their coach did they have the Competency and/or Willingness needed?

Name:	Competency (Yes or No?)	Willingness (Yes or No?)
1. _____	____	____
2. _____	____	____
3. _____	____	____
4. _____	____	____
5. _____	____	____

Once you've determined the levels of *Competency* and/or *Willingness* of the individual staff members, then the appropriate coaching approach for that person and situation should be applied. The coaching approach determines your level of participation when helping your staff member to improve.

Following are the Coaching Approaches and the managers' level of participation:

A. *Inform:*

<u>Evaluate:</u>   Determine and communicate what you want done and ask for timelines.
(Don't tell them how, they already know)

<u>Discover:</u>   Allow them to determine their own objectives and obstacles.

<u>Plan:</u>   Allow them to develop action plans.

<u>Implement:</u>   Allow them to tack action on their own.
1.   Keep communication open
2.   Praise often
3.   Challenge their abilities

B. *Instruct:*

<u>Evaluate:</u>   Determine and communicate what you want done and by when.

<u>Discover:</u>   Help them to understand reasons, causes and objectives.

<u>Plan:</u>   Jointly develop a plan.

<u>Implement:</u>   Facilitate actions closely.
(Keep communications open and praise initiative)

C. *Inspire:*

Evaluate: Determine and communicate what you want done.
(If needed: Jointly determine causes for lack of Will)
(Jointly identify need for improvement. Help them to clearly understand needs and expectations)

Discover: Jointly uncover causes for improvement needs.
(Approach as if they possess both Skill and Will)
(Jointly determine objectives.)

Plan: Jointly develop Plan
(Provide clear and measurable expectations)

Implement: Supervise closely, Inspect outcomes, Praise initiative

D. *Involve:*

<u>Evaluate:</u> Determine and communicate what you want done.
(Make sure your expectations are clear)
(If possible, help them understand the importance of the need)

<u>Discover:</u> Communicate why these things should be done.
(If possible, help them understand the value of the tasks)

<u>Plan:</u> Communicate how you want it done and by when.
(Question them to make sure they know how)
(Assign specific time frames for task completion)

<u>Implement:</u> Provide specific reporting and communication Guidelines
(Requires supervision, communication and involvement)
(Praise follow-through and task completion)

Exercise:

In your opinion which Coaching Approach is needed for each of your team members most often? *(Inform, Instruct, Inspire or Involve)*

Name:	Approach	Name:	Approach
_____		_____	
_____		_____	
_____		_____	
_____		_____	

Conclusions:

All of the other topics discussed and reviewed in this book are important pieces of the staff member developmental puzzle, but the catalyst with which we ignite improvement is timely, effective, and appropriate coaching

A managers' responsibility is greater than simply communicating expectations and information. In fact, the successful managers whom I've met believe that we all have the responsibility to lead, encourage, and develop our staff members toward improvement.

How successful would any sports team or any individual player be without a great coach? Why then do some managers seem to believe that by telling employees what is expected of them that their staff members should always be able to lift themselves up to the higher levels of expectation and achievement without assistance? We all need a little help from time to time, don't we?

Determine what coaching approach is needed for your staff member the next time he/ she needs help, then apply the appropriate techniques for that situation and watch how quickly they improve. You'll most likely be pleasantly surprised.

Staff members want to know that someone cares about them and their work. Show them that you do...coach them!

Chapter Ten

A Disconnected Reality!

Mistake #8   *Being in conflict with other departments.*

How are interdepartmental communications and relationships in your company? I'm always a little fascinated, whenever I ask this question in a workshop, I see eyes roll, hear deep sighs. I see glances at the floor and breath held, as if some people are waiting for the other shoe to drop. And then, as if the appropriate words have been taught in some politically correct success school someone inevitably says, "It could be better."

It could be better? Somehow, based on the reaction I frequently get when I ask this question, I have to wonder what "It could be better" really means.

I've discovered that at least some of the interdepartmental communication and relationship problems stem from what I call a, *Disconnected Reality* A *Disconnected Reality* is a perception that is true for the person who believes it, but which is untrue in the minds of most others around them. As examples, I often meet sales managers who say that most of their largest problems come from the service and support departments. Meanwhile, if you ask any group of service and support managers what is the source of their problems, they in almost musical unison will sing, "the sales department!" Some of the sales, service, and support managers today also seem to be convinced that many senior managers have completely lost touch with reality, and in some cases the true everyday issues, and that this is where many of their problems come from! Can they all be right? Is it possible that the only person that really knows what is going on and what needs to be done is the person with the opinion? And should it always be done *their* way? This is a *Disconnected Reality*.

Where do these feelings come from, and even more importantly, how can it affect the decisions that a manager makes in their everyday work life?

When I was a young salesperson I had issues. (O.K., so I still have issues, but not the ones that I talk about in this little book.) One of my issues was that I had a strong belief that nothing should be more important than the customer. Moreover, the customer and *I* were always right. Because of this belief structure, I was known on many occasions to pick up the *banner of cause* and literally run into another department waiving my banner and uncovering the wrong doings of others in the way they approached their jobs. Of course, I believed that, since I was a top producing salesperson, they should listen to me and follow my instructions. At least that was the way I saw it. Oddly enough, very few other people saw things the way I did. In fact, (and I found this hard to believe), most of them thought that I was the problem. Can you believe it? I was the problem? This was my *Disconnected Reality*.

Well you can imagine the outcome. Not only did my customers and I not receive the help for which I was looking, but I also recognized over a period of time that my customers were actually receiving less attention and concern than some other salespeople's customers. Go figure! Do you happen to know anyone else who occasionally spends, time, energy, and effort in areas that they have no control, influence, or sometimes…business? Do you know anyone who occasionally approaches another department or employee with an inappropriate attitude or point of view? Or am I the only one that has been previously caught in this unlikely situation? I think not.

Over time I learned that my own *disconnected reality* was causing, not solving, problems. I finally understood that we are all on the same team. I learned that the managers in other departments, and in most cases their staff, were professional adults who, like me, were doing the best they could to make the right decisions, at the right time, for the right reasons. My decisions to be in conflict with other departments and not work with and through them caused my customers and me to suffer. I'm certainly glad that I had a mentor who helped me figure out what I did wrong before I became a manager. Did you?

 ### Situation:

Maria manages a telephony environment sales and customer service team, both inbound and outbound, for a national telecommunications company. Her office is located in Houston. Her department is responsible for sales in addition to the initial processing of new orders and connects. Plus, her staff is the front line contact for any customer connection problems that may arise with the new accounts. Maria has several years of industry experience, and she has seen dozens of changes in technology and procedures over the years. The latest change by her company has been a reorganization of responsibilities, which now expects her department to be responsible for new customer complaints. The company has also centralized final order processing to the district office in Dallas. These changes have caused a bevy of problems in Maria's department. Still, she has in her words, "taken the bull by the horns." She's beginning to make a name for herself at the district office as someone who "won't take no for an answer." She's also making a name with her staff as someone who will "go to the mat" to get things straightened out when one of her employees needs her help.

Over the last few weeks, Maria's team has found it more and more difficult to get a timely response from any of their new contacts at the district processing center, and Maria has told her employees on several occasions that "things are pretty messed-up over there!"

Decisions:

This morning, two of her outbound reps came to her and said that they have had a problem processing orders "again," and that they didn't get any help through the appropriate channels. They also told her that they are tired of the "constant battle," and they wanted to know what, if anything, could be done about their issues. Maria decides to take matters into her own hands. She comments, "if she ran her department the way *those people* do, nothing would get sold or done." She tells her executive assistant to get the manager of the processing department on the phone, now!

Complications:

Once Maria gets Larry, the manager of the district processing department, on the phone she tells Larry that she is extremely disappointed in his staff's apparent "lack of ability" to solve simple problems and do their jobs. Her two employees, still sitting in her office, are apparently enjoying the scene. She lets him know that her customers and her staff have been inconvenienced enough by the procedural changes that the company has made and the very least Larry could do is to make sure his employees give the highest level of support when her people call with a problem that was no doubt created by Larry's team of "would be professionals!"

Consequences:

Now the tables turn. Larry, grabbing an opportunity to get a word in edge-wise, tells Maria that he has already compiled a list of incomplete or incorrect orders by her team, and that this list is "a mile long." He tells her that the complaints about her and her team make their way to his office several times a day. He also mentions that her team seems to have a total disregard for the work, effort and results that his people take such careful pains to produce. Larry then tells Maria that her department is the only team in the whole district with which he has these kinds of problems or complaints, and that rather than finishing this "useless" conversation with her he's now going to hang up and march directly over to the District Vice President's office to see how she feels about this situation and how it should be handled! "Click!" Wow! I wonder if Maria's employees could hear any of that? Do you think that Maria will receive the assistance that she was looking for to help her team? Do you think that the V.P. will be in situational agreement with Maria or Larry? I'll bet that Maria's boss will have an opinion about her ability to manage relationships with her people and other departments. In fact, most of her staff's poor interdepartmental relations were most likely influenced and encouraged by Maria's unprofessional approaches, behaviors and comments.

Strategy:

Many of my students and I have learned that in our zealousness to do what we feel is right, we sometimes do what is wrong. Any decision that leads you or your team to be in conflict with other departments instead of working with and through them to find solutions will most likely be the wrong decision. A decision that may leave you in conflict with the boss is also an inappropriate decision. Doesn't the boss need to feel comfortable with your skills as a manager and decision maker? What could happen if he/ she is not? Also, in Maria's case, any decision to make negative comments about other departments to her team and possibly influence negative attitudes and behaviors from them is definitely the wrong decision. Wouldn't you agree?

In order to find the appropriate decision-making approach we need to work from an introspective perspective.

The key concept to eliminate situations like Maria's in the future is *positive influence. Positive influence is earned.* Some managers believe that because they are a manager that other people, even other departments are supposed to respect, listen to and follow their directions simply because they currently fill the role of manager. One example of this is when a new manager is given the responsibility for a team and then begins to behave as if everyone that they talk to should do as they're told. Some may do as they're told for a while, but eventually people will begin to resist this new manager's orders because if you want respect you must earn respect by offering respect. Long-term *positive influence* is earned in a similar fashion. If the appropriate relationships are to be constructed and positive influence is to be exerted with other departments, then we need to take a long and introspective look at what *we* are doing before we concern ourselves too much about what *they* are doing.

One of the things that may help us to understand what could encourage Maria to make inappropriate decisions in these situations is to understand that whenever a manager begins to feel a loss of *control* in their environment, they may sometimes attempt to exert *force* instead of *influence*. I don't mean physical force. I mean verbal force. Some managers who find themselves in this situation may attempt to overpower another person verbally rather than utilize influence with them. With all of the changes that managers must sell, implement, and endure these days, it has become more and more common for them to feel a loss of control. If we have these feelings, then how we deal with them, and the decisions that we make during these times may very well determine our longer-term relationships with our staff, other departments, and our bosses. Allow me to ask this: how do you feel when someone attempts to verbally *over power* you? Most people don't care for it very much.

Let's begin our strategy this way; you may be familiar with Stephen Covey's *"The Seven Habits of Highly Effective People."* In this book, he makes reference to a person's *circle of influence* as it relates to being more proactive. He also writes about *direct* and *indirect* influence as it relates to other areas of life. I'd like you to consider a similar strategic point of view, but with a slightly different tactical approach.

There are certain things in our environment and lives that we can *Control.*

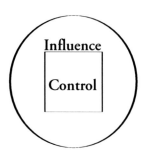

Outside of our area of control, there is an even larger area of situations and things that we can't control, but over which we do have *Influence.* Many people have called this our *circle of influence.* By the way, I've found that most managers have much more influence than for which they give themselves true credit.

Outside of our area of *Influence*, there is an even larger area of situations and things over which we have *No Control* and very little or no influence.

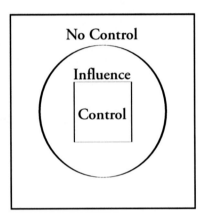

I've determined that what helps many people to understand positive, proactive, and productive decision-making in these common areas of work and life is to simply remember some short, but extremely important attitude concepts that apply to each of these three areas.

Area # 1: Control

There are two words that we should remember in our personal area of control. The two words are *Do it!* If in your opinion, something needs to be done and you believe that it might be in an area of your control, then *Do it*. Don't procrastinate, don't hesitate and don't wait *Do it*. According to many of the successful people with whom I've worked, one of the leading causes of stress in business today is procrastination. In an effort to prevent it, if the task is something that you think is in an area of your control, and you believe that it needs to be done… then *Do it*.

Area #2: Influence

There are two words that we should remember in our personal area of influence. These two crucial words are *Be nice!* If you think that something needs to be done and you attempt to do it, but you find that you can't or shouldn't because it's really in someone else's area of control then, *Be nice.* If you find that someone else must be enlisted to handle the situation, whatever it is, *Be nice.* Consider this; when you have experienced someone coming to you for assistance, and they're *not* being nice, are you more or less likely to want to help? Many people will say, "I'd be less likely to help." So it stands to reason that if you need or want someone else's help then, *Be nice.*

Area #3: No Control

In the area over which we have no control, the three important words to remember are *Get over it!* Contrary to the beliefs of some, I'm not attempting to be difficult when I suggest getting over it; I'm being practical. Think about it. If you attempt to control anything, but you find that control is not possible, or if you attempt to influence something, but you determine that you can't, then *Get over it.* If you know going into a situation that historically you haven't been able to control or influence it, even if you don't like it, *Get over it.*

You will find it more difficult to improve your position in most relationships if you spend too much time attempting to exert control or influence in areas over which you have none. The reason that you may not be able to have control or influence is most likely because it's in someone else's area of control or influence. So, what are you doing in there anyway? *Get over it.* How much business and work time is wasted by employees and managers in situational areas in which they should never become involved in the first place. Based on what I've seen and heard, it happens quite often. So do yourself and others a favor, *Get over it!*

Doesn't all of this make common sense? Maybe your thinking, "Well, that sounds right, but what about Jack? He's the manager in that other department and he's been disagreeable with me as long as I've known him. Does this approach really apply to the interaction that I have with Jack?" "Do I have to be nice?" Or, "What about when the company or senior management does something that I simply don't believe is right? Should I just get over it?"

Consider this possible answer to the second question. If you think that something needs changing, and it's out of your control. Be nice. You can continue to exert influence until the boss says, *Get over it,* then, if you value your relationship with the boss...you should probably what? You guessed it. Get over it. By the way, if you intend to have the best influence in any situation then be prepared with the appropriate data. Maria was making decisions and having conversations based on emotion. Larry was making decisions and having a conversation based on collected data. The boss is always more likely to listen to and believe in logical, collected, analyzed data.

As it relates to the question of being nice to Jack, even if Jack has always been difficult, be nice! I will offer you some special insight. Something I learned a long time ago and which I've found it to be proven true time and time again is *Change the way you feel and act toward others, and watch how quickly they change the way they feel and act toward you!* In every difficult business relationship someone's going to need to make the first mature, professional, relationship building gesture. Why shouldn't it be you? Besides, someone needs to be the *team builder.* Hmmm…isn't team building more productive than ego building? So, even if it's Jack, be nice.

Conclusions:

My recommendations:

Exercise:

Make a list of all of the most important issues, concerns, or problems with which you're currently faced. Then, attempt to determine whether they are in an area of *Control, Influence,* or *No Control.* Mark them with the appropriate corresponding letter.

(Keep in mind that you may find later that you've inadvertently put them in the wrong area. That's O.K.! Just change.)

Issue, Concern or Problem	(C)ontrol, (I)nfluence or (N)o Control
1.) _____	_____
2.) _____	_____
3.) _____	_____
4.) _____	_____
5.) _____	_____

Once you've completed your list it's time to take action. Just remember the important words discussed previously, "Do it, Be nice or Get over it!"

If your beginning list is longer than 5 (five) items don't worry. You know that you have plenty to do already, so simply prioritize. If you determine that some of the items are in an area of "No Control" then "Get over it" for now, and go on to the next item.

Finally, remember to approach people with whom you intend to have influence with a *selling attitude.* Why is it that we so often attempt to *sell* people that we don't really know very well on our ideas, concerns and needs, and then with those people that should mean the most to us or are in the best situation to help us, we attempt to *tell* them what they should do? Have you ever noticed this? Remember, people would rather be sold than told. Here's how we do that.

4 Steps to a "Selling" Attitude

*S*eek to understand *their* concerns.
*E*nhance your understanding of *their* perspective.
*L*earn *their* language!
*L*isten for more opportunity!

    1.)   *S*eek to understand *their* concerns.

Everyone has his or her own concerns, issues and problems. Do you recall *WIIFM?* Attempt to understand from where they're coming. In order to be a good salesperson and sell them on cooperation, you need to attempt to understand and care about *their* needs. If you can get the help or outcome that you're looking for and at the same time help them to better their current situation, shouldn't their help come much more willingly and quickly?

2.) <u>Enhance your understanding of *their* perspective.</u>

Ask questions and listen to the complete answers. Not allowing someone to voice their opinions and concerns will not help you sell them. Cutting them off before they finish explaining their perspectives will only convince them that you really don't care and in return possibly leave you wanting for important information. When they ask a question, listen to the whole question. When they answer a question, listen to the whole answer. Help them to continue to openly communicate with you. Ask good questions. *Remember: You can always tell when a conversation is over. Someone stops talking!*

3.) <u>Learn *their* language!</u>

Once you determine the approach that you think would best serve your goals and theirs, then present your approach in the other person's language. What's the boss's language? Is it the results? Whatever is most important to the person with whom you're speaking, that's *their* language. Learn their language, and talk to them in terms that they think are important. Remember that just because you feel that something is important doesn't mean that everyone else feels or even should feel the same way.

4.) <u>Listen for more opportunity!</u>

Building a great relationship is done over time. Listen for opportunities to help the other person achieve their goals and solve their problems. The more help that you offer over time, the more likely you'll find someone receptive when you need help. I've heard that the only true way to get what you want out of life is to help other people get what they want. Have you heard that? Listen for those opportunities to help, and then if you can, help them.

There's an old acronym for the word TEAM. *Together Everyone Achieves More!* We're all on the same team. Our staff, our customers, and we are best served when we all become a cooperative, positive, and powerful unit. Let's do the best we can to work with, and through, other departments. Let's watch out for, and if possible, avoid or improve any *Disconnected Realities.* I'm sure that you'll find, like so many others, that the relationships and the payoffs are well worth the effort!

Chapter Eleven

The Human Resource

Mistake #9   Turning good employees into ex-employees.

Years ago, I began my sales career in a very competitive business. There was not only competition with other companies in our industry, but there was heavy competition between sales teams, and salespeople within our own company. I remember that there were certain things in our company that could have gotten me fired. If you showed up late for work two times in the same month you would have been fired. If you missed a sales meeting or didn't keep a complete customer/ prospect log you could have gotten fired. For general house cleaning purposes the bottom three people on the sales productivity board were fired every month.

I remember the employee conversations and their perceptions, which suggested that the company and its managers only cared about themselves. I remember that these employee perspective conversations also included discussions regarding the lack of respect that the company and its managers had for their employees because there were no support, training or developmental processes in place in any department to help a good employee keep up or get ahead. As many were told, it was all up to the employee to "work it out" if they developed a productivity problem. Normally, when one of these little complaint sessions would get far enough along, someone would step in an say something like, "You know in a company as successful as ours it's not very difficult to find replacements." "Maybe we should get back to work." Someone in the group would agree, and back to work we would all go.

Unemployment was at an all time high during that period of time. Back then the U.S. recession, the gasoline crises, inflation, and other influences were taking a toll on American businesses. Many people that were fortunate enough to find good jobs attempted to stay in them and hoped that they didn't get laid off.

My father and mother both retired from a major electronics design and manufacturing company, and I believe that it's the only job that my father ever had during his adult life. I remember being told by many adults when I was growing up that "a good education and a good job, with a good company is what life was all about!" Have things changed or what? When I was a young employee, if you interviewed for a job and over the last ten years had more than two previous jobs, the interviewer was likely to think that you were "unstable" or a "job hopper." Today, if you apply for a job, and you've been at the same job for the last ten years, the interviewer is likely to ask about, or at least wonder, why you have become so stagnant. "Are you an underachiever" they may wonder? Wow! Have things changed.

Situation:

Lane is a District Sales Manager for a large pharmaceutical company. He is responsible for twenty-three outside sales reps that cover six states in the Midwest. Lane by reputation is a *closer*. Lane's team makes the quarterly number. Lane's people do what they are told. Lane has been known to say, "If you want a team to respect you, then you have to keep a firm grip on the reins." and Lane keeps a firm grip. Everyone is required to e-mail a daily activity report to Lane's office no later than 6:30 pm every day. Everyone is required to let Lane know where each of their prospects and customers are in the sales pipeline so he can schedule his field time according to the need for closing deals. Lane has work procedures that better be followed, or else. These measures include quarterly meetings to be attended, projection reports, workday schedules and time frames, and the introduction of Lane to all of the primary decision makers for every major account. Why does he have these regulations? Well according to Lane, no one can get the *whole* deal the same way he can. Everyday he instructs his staff where they should go, what they should say, and what they should be able to accomplish when they get there. Lane then shows up where he believes that he is most needed and useful. Usually he shows up to *close* something.

Lane has also been known to "lay down the law" if someone doesn't do as well as he would expect. The reason that he insists on meeting all the major account decision makers is because that Lane believes that there's no employee loyalty to the company any more. According to Lane, "higher turnover is just the way it is these days." In his mind this must be true because turnover on his team has never been higher. Of course a few of Lane's exiting employees have told him that they are either "bored with their jobs" or that they "don't like being micro-managed." Lane has simply told them that, "It's my way, or the highway! What I do makes money for people. Make a choice." Lane discounts their comments as a lack of "commitment to the job." And he says that, "they just don't make employees the way that they used to."

Decisions:

Lane's Regional V.P. has concerns. He's looked over the numbers and it appears that Lane is developing a problem. Yes, it's easy to see that Lane's team makes the *top line* plan but the cost of turnover on Lane's team makes the *bottom line* a weak, and it appears to be getting worse as time goes by. The V.P. has a meeting with Lane. He reminds Lane that the combined hard and soft costs of losing an employee in their company in the first three to six months averages about $46,000. Turnover on Lane's team is higher than the other two District Sales Manager's turnover put together. Lane turned over 9 employees last year and has already lost 10 employees in the first 3 quarters of this year. According to the V.P., those are "big hits" to take on the bottom line! Lane attempts to defend himself and his decisions by telling the V.P. that, "he doesn't create the holes he just fills them." The V.P. responds by telling Lane that, "he had better figure out where the *holes* are and *plug* them, or come the end of the year he may need to *evaluate* Lane's position with the company."

It sounds to me like Lane better do some evaluating himself, and quickly. What to you think? Have you ever known a manager like Lane? I hope not, but I'm sure that some people will say they have.

Lane decides, in his words, "to make his team more money." His assumption is that if he works harder and helps them close even more deals that they will make more money, become happier and stay longer. What do you think? Is that what you would assume? Will Lane's decision improve the obvious lack of desire to stay around that seems to develop with common regularity on his team? Probably not.

Complications

Over the next three months, Lane works harder than ever, and he requires his team does the same. He promises his salespeople that he's going to make them more money than they've ever made before. He seems to have meticulous enthusiasm for his processes. He runs to the field to help improve the conditions of every possible sale. Because of Lane's decisions and actions, top line revenue goes up by 13% for his team. Unfortunately, because of the added expenses of Lane's travel, commission expenses, and the fact that he lost two more people, amongst other things, his teams' bottom line is in worse shape this quarter than it was last quarter. Oops!

Consequences:

It's time for the toll of Lane's decisions to be paid. Although, for many managers, Lane's decisions and actions are easy to understand, and to some extent, they may even empathize with him. I've seen quite a few managers over the years make decisions about how to help their staff get recommitted to the job based on *top line* achievement and disregard the *bottom line* consequences of their decisions. Still, time has taught us that we can't ignore the common outcomes of decisions like Lane's.

Haven't you seen people in your own business or industry leave their job and go somewhere else for reasons other than money? Don't people work at their particular job for other reasons than just money? According to the successful leaders and managers with whom I've worked, the answer is yes! People also work for what I call *Gratification Income.*

Gratification Income is more than just money, and it can be a little different for each person. We each hope to support ourselves and our loved ones in a lifestyle that we feel will be reasonable, and so to some extent money is important. But even that hope is more than dollars and cents alone. The lifestyle that we hope to provide our family is about the quality of life that we hope to afford. Still, there are other reasons why people stay and work hard at a job. What are some of your other reasons for remaining in your position? What? You don't think you have any? Allow me to ask these questions: if you had to struggle everyday with work protocols that you thought were demeaning might you start looking for another job? If you felt that you were truly unappreciated by your boss might you consider discontinuing your employment? If you were never allowed to grow or develop as an employee or a person, and were only allowed to do the same boring tasks everyday on the job, even if you made good money, might you at some point look into other employment options? Oddly enough, when I ask these questions in workshops the answer I often get is yes. I even had a few attending students say, "I did leave!"

As for Lane, the consequences that he faces include a demotion. The V.P. decides that, "Lane doesn't understand the way the world, business and people function today." So Lane is given the opportunity to go out and do what he has proven to be best at…selling pharmaceuticals.

Strategy:

The real cure here lies in realigning Lane's employee perspectives. One perspective that Lane seems to have is that no one but he is competent to make decisions. There's a difference between being aware of your staff's daily activities and telling them what to do. Telling employees what to do, but not helping them develop better decision making skills is commonly known as *micro-management.* Something that I think Lane's ex-employees attempted to point out to him once or twice. Do you think that maybe Lane wasn't listening? Effective and prudent delegation is an important key to staff member competency development . And what about effective coaching? We discussed the value of effective coaching in chapter nine, *Improvement Coaching.* Doesn't that also help to improve tenure and create happier, more productive staff members?

For those of you that are parents…how will our children ever learn to make effective decisions, if we never allow them to make a decision? If your employees are not allowed to grow and develop on the job, might they become bored or unhappy and consider looking elsewhere for employment? Besides, don't many employees today believe that they are most likely going to be looking for another job at some point in their career? Wouldn't that same employee value learning and experiencing as much as possible in their current role or position so that they then may be worth more when they apply for their next job? What do you think? We as managers and leaders of others have a responsibility to grow and develop our employees, even to the possible end of loosing them to a better job opportunity. Of course the reality of this attitude about empowering our staff is that the better we meet this responsibility the longer most employees stay with us.

We discussed recurring problems in *Proactive Possibilities*. Do you think that at some point Lane should have recognized that he had some recurring problems and proactively considered making some different decisions and possibly taking some different actions? Lane's actions prove that he is either unaware or uncaring of these recurring issues.

Next, what about Lane's perspective that what his people want most out of their job and their relationship with him is more money? How much will you put up with for more money? And how long will you endure it? We all have our own plans and desires for our future. Lane seemed to think that everyone should see things the same way - his way. Is that realistic? It would have made more common sense for him to spend a little more time getting to know what was important to each individual employee and working with him or her to help that person achieve those things? *Gratification Income* can be different for each of us. We all have our own reasons for what we do, or don't do. Lane should have paid a little closer attention to what each staff member really wanted. My mother used to say, "God gave us two ears and one mouth for a reason." Once again I think mom was right. I think that if Lane had done a little more responsible listening and a little less unresponsive telling he and his team could have been a lot better off.

Finally, let's examine Lane's perspective of the team's responsibility picture. His team's responsibility picture appeared to be too small. His focus was on the *top line* number instead of the *bottom line* results that his boss attempted to share with him. His focus was on the top line of daily activity rather than the bottom line of productivity with his people's behaviors and developmental outcomes. Rather than focusing on the bottom line of individual and team development he focused on the top line of increasing sales. The sad thing is that if Lane had been a little more focused on the effective priorities of team management and leadership, he could have used some of his profound selling skills to sell in order to develop his people, improve tenure, and reduce expenses to achieve levels of success that everyone could truly appreciate. By the way, don't you think that the top line might have been improved naturally if the high quality men and women improved on Lane's team had stayed on the job longer?

Let's look at what should be done.

(Three steps to improving tenure with our "Human Resource")

1.) Be more sensitive to our staff members' motivation.

I don't mean that we need be more *"touchy-feely"* sensitive. I mean that we need to be more pro-actively aware of what the individual would like to get from the experience of their job and then help them to achieve it. We need to understand more clearly their individual *motivations.*

2.) Consider being a little more flexible with staff member responsibilities

Some employees accept responsibility more quickly than others. Allow those staff members who want it to have it. Processes in business are important, but they shouldn't be inflexible to individual employee desire for improvement and development. Processes should complement improvement and development. Responsibility on the job means *decision-making.* Help those that want to make decisions make the right ones with your developmental influences. Understand that people develop at different speeds and be *flexible* and supportive of each employee's responsibility growth rate.

3.) Help staff members to see the Big Picture and get connected to it.

Many employees today want to feel that they are part of something greater than only themselves. What is the mission of your company and your team? How do staff members *fit* into the *big picture*? Do you have plans for the team and each individual staff member? How do team plans and staff member development plans connect in the scheme of things? Once you've created your plans and helped your employees make these connections shouldn't we help them to develop their own plans? When an employee begins to see where they fit into the big picture they begin to focus on individual improvement and development plans. Then they stay longer; and why shouldn't they? They *are* more likely to get what they need and want.

Exercise: How well do you know your team?

Write down the name of one of your employees on a separate sheet of paper. Then, number the page 1 – 10 down the left hand side and answer each of these questions about the individual employee. *(Attempt this exercise solely from your current base of knowledge.)*

1.) Why do they come to work?
2.) Why do they work for you?
3.) What do they want from the company and/ or the job?
4.) What do they expect from your relationship with them?
5.) How did they feel about their last job and boss?
6.) How do they see their future in your company? In the world?

7.) What dreams do they have for themselves and/or their family?

8.) How do they feel about the other members of their team?

9.) How do they think you feel about them?

10.) How do they feel about you as a manager, a leader, a coach?

(Once you've completed this with one of your employees, repeat the exercise with the name of each of the other members of your team. Remember, these answers should come from you, not from them.)

What did you learn from this exercise? In your opinion, would your perspective and your staff's perspective be in alignment? Are you in need of a little more information? Let's explore how you might attain more information.

Conclusions:

Before you start grilling your employees under the inquisition spot lights to get their answers to the questions in the previous exercise, allow me to offer a couple of suggestions.

First, the best time to get to know more about your staff is when you are working with them. Whether your working with them in the field, or in the office, you can gain a lot of special insight into what an employee is all about if you simply watch and listen a little more and do and talk a little less. Part of a manager's staff member development responsibilities is to encourage the employee to want to develop. Sometimes for the sake of improvement, we're going to need to call on employees to do things that are difficult or distasteful for them. The more that we know about what motivates them on the job, the easier it will be to motivate and encourage them to improve themselves when the time comes. Most of the employees that I've spoken with seem to have an appreciation for at least one manager in their past who helped them to become more than they thought capable.

Second, we must help our employees to develop individual goals and improvement plans on the job. Today, more than ever, it is likely that an employee may become lost or disgruntled in the waves of change and improvements that companies are required to make in order to survive and thrive in the marketplace. If we don't help our employees to get *connected* to their own *big picture* then we run a greater risk of allowing the staff member to loose sight of their own future inside our company. By helping them to connect, we help them understand why and to whom the work they do is so important. The work they do is important for their loved ones, their customers, their company, for you and for them. Let's help them to see and understand the importance of their good work.

It's not uncommon today for a staff member to come to work and announce, "I'm not going to be here very long." Some managers can become concerned that this *threat* of leaving will in some way harm the employee, the company, or even the team. In contrast, I have heard many employees make the statement, "I'm not going to be here very long" only to stay on the job for years. Why? I might suggest that they stayed because most often when they went to work they got what they needed and wanted from the job. So, why leave?

Consider this…even if an employee's previous experience suggests to them that they probably won't get what they are looking for from you or the job. Or even if they truly believe that at some point they are probably going to become so disappointed, disgruntled or bored that they may want to leave, I say, "as long as it's not today." When staff members come to work and get what they want and need today, they'll most likely be back tomorrow. Great working relationships have always been based on how we behave today. Help you staff to go home everyday feeling as if each day is a great day for them!

Many resources are required for a manager to become and remain successful on the job today. Let's not forget about or take too lightly our most powerful and beneficial resource, our *Human Resource*. Because without them…well…can you get all the work done yourself? The short cut to greater levels of team performance has always been the high quality men and women that stay, work and improve. Help staff members to want to stay.

Chapter Twelve

Leading By Example

Mistake #10   Believing that "Leadership" is about getting "other people" to do something.

Have you ever heard the phrase *"Lead by example?"* We probably all have. We all know that leading by example in its purest sense is a good thing, but the appropriate *pre-leading* question needs to be answered. That question is, *"By what example do you lead?"* If your example is, "I'm the first one in the office in the morning and the last one to leave at night." is that the best example by which to lead? Oh yea, that's what your staff members want to be when they grow up…TIRED!

Others seem to believe that *leading by example* means mustering the appropriate amount of enthusiasm for important tasks or goals that need to be achieved and then inspiring the people on their team to "go forth and conquer!" Inspiring others to action is a valuable talent. Achieving objectives in anything, especially business, is certainly important but these things are not the true essence, purpose, or action of great leadership. When managers begin to believe that leadership is about getting other people to do something, they begin taking themselves and their teams down a very challenging road.

When we experience the privilege of contact with a great leader, we may also encounter a large group of people following this leader and say to ourselves, "What power he/ she must possess!" "How charismatic and intelligent this leader must be. How successful they must be in order to get such a wonderful group of people to follow them!" I have been told by some managers that they have worked for someone who was a great leader, but they feel they could never be as great a leader as that person because they don't possess the same vibrant personality, or some other qualities that they think are important for leadership and often aren't.

Still others believe that you can be born to be a leader. I spent a few years in the military, and this was the perspective they taught. I have to admit; I'm not buying that philosophy either. I've seen the character of leadership in the most unlikely places and from the most unlikely people. Maybe you have as well. Besides, I've never seen a birth announcement in the newspaper that read, "Mr. And Mrs. John Smith have given birth to a 7lb 6oz…leader!" Have you? No, the paper normally says, "boy or girl."

So the essence of leadership and the qualities which promote good leadership can be confusing can't it? Allow me to shed a little light on leadership.

Situation:

Mary Beth is the sales manager of an advertising sales team. She works for a nationally distributed magazine. She's had the job for a relatively short time. She replaced her boss Joe, who retired five months ago. In Mary Beth's opinion, Joe was a great Sales Manager. He was a great leader. He seemed to have a way of making the large problems that the team encountered appear less threatening. He could always guide, direct, and motivate the people on his team to get the job done, even when the real pressure was on. He never let the pressures of sale's quotas or increasing expectations for productivity infringe on the spirit or the morale of the team. Joe had a way of making and offering decisions that seemed to encourage everyone's belief and trust in him. Everyone seemed to be happy because they were part of Joe's team. The staff simply enjoyed being around him. Mary Beth has large shoes to fill, and she knows it.

Things went pretty well on Mary Beth's team for the first two or three months. The truth is that there was about 2 months worth of *spill over* business that had been pipelined while Joe was still there. When Mary Beth took over as manager, she jumped right in and did many of the things that she had seen Joe do. She held regular team meetings to talk about where the team was in terms of objectives and what each team member needed to do. She processed the paperwork of the department and used it to let her people know what they should and shouldn't be doing every day. She even went into the field a couple of times to help close a deal. One of the more difficult deals, one that the sales rep thought was lost she actually saved. The sales rep might have closed the deal without her, but she felt that if she hadn't gotten involved it might not have made as large a profit, and she also calculated that her performance had given her a great opportunity to shine in front of her team. She remembers thinking, "Boy, I can get a lot of mileage out of telling the story of that *save* around the office, everyone would have to respect me now!"

Over time Mary Beth got more and more caught up in the processes of her job. She knew that Joe used to spend more *one on one* time with the salespeople, but he'd been doing the job for years. And, because of his tenure with the company he probably wasn't as closely watched and directed as she has been over the last few months. Mary Beth *did* begin to experience one thing that she had never seen Joe experience. She felt the pains of the end of the month *crunch*. The expectation of higher sales quotas had put her team in a crunch to achieve the number. "Did Joe ever have to deal with this?" she wondered. "I don't remember it if he did," she said to herself. "Oh well, I'll just pump them up in the next team meeting, and we'll be fine."

<u>**Decisions:**</u>

The pressure of the increased quota was wearing on her. She had been a little curt with a couple of the people on her staff, but surely they understood that there was tremendous pressure on her as the manager of the team. Mary Beth couldn't quite put her finger on why it was happening, but she knew that she was loosing productivity and relationship ground. Her team *had* made quota the two previous months, but it was way too close. The team also appeared a little edgy, and she was not sure why. Several of the people on her team seemed to be less motivated than they should have been. Also, everyone seemed to have less confidence in her than they had with Joe. They began to question some of her directions and decisions. She had experience. She had talent. She had the job. Senior management had seen fit to make her the team leader, so what was the problem? Mary Beth knew that she needed to do something to get productivity up, so she made the decision to have another real *fire'em up and get'em going* sales meeting…she'd seen Joe do it, and it always worked for him. She was sure that she could convince her team to do what she wanted and needed them to do.

Do you think that Mary Beth was missing some things? Don't you think that if Joe was so respected, motivating, and willingly followed by his team that there may have been some other things that he was doing? There is more to leading people to greater achievement than enthusiastic meetings and motivational speeches. The truly successful leaders, with whom I've had the privilege to spend time, believe this to be true.

<u>**Complications:**</u>

Mary Beth's team made their monthly objective but not without a certain amount of concern and trial. The *rumblings* on the team, according to Mary Beth had turned to *tremors* and she even had an *earthquake* with one of her staff members. Marcus told Mary Beth that he, and some of the others, were "getting tired of her last minute pump up sessions" and wanted to know "when she was going to do some actual work" that would help the team? Mary wondered where this lack of respect had come from and thought, "Is it my age?" "Is it my lack of management time on the job?" "Is it because I'm a woman?" "Is it because Joe had been with the team for so long?"

Mary Beth decided that a real leader would face these threats to the team head on. She decided to have an emergency meeting with the team and do a check-up from the neck up to find out who and what the real problems were and to let the team know just how hard she had been working. She also let them know that she didn't appreciate the apparent "behind her back conversations" that had been taking place and reminded them that they would have never treated Joe that way! She's right on at least the last point. They probably wouldn't have thought of or treated Joe the same. Do you know why?

Consequences:

Things eventually fall apart for Mary Beth. Her team begins to become less consistent in their monthly achievement. Over the next few months, three of her team goes to work for a competitor and she believes that she's going to need to fire another because he can't seem to get the job done and his attitude has become a problem. Mary Beth seems to have less *happy* meetings with her team these days, and she spends most of her team meeting time asking why they're not doing what they know they should do. A friend that works for another company tells her that it's fairly common to be faced with rebuilding a team after a long time manager leaves. Do you believe that her friend's statement is necessarily true?

Poor Mary Beth. She started with the best intentions, but she received some of the worst outcomes. Have you ever seen anything like this before?

Strategy:

Even though the final cure to Mary Beth's decision-making problems may appear quite complicated, I think that you'll find the answer, once we get there, quite simple.

Let's examine Mary Beth's attitudes, perceptions, and decisions. Mary Beth believed that leadership was about what she could get others to do. Consider her decisions for herself and her staff along the path to team disintegration. Let's examine the examples that she was leading by.

Mary Beth's Decisions:

A.) *Focusing more on the daily and monthly activities of her job than on the people on her team.*

This is a common mistake made by new leaders. Like Mary Beth, a new leader may assume that the staff member's need for individual focus and development will wait while she gets her feet on the ground in her new job. Couldn't this send the message to staff members that we care more about our new job than we do about them? When Mary Beth did spend time with the team in meetings, what did she talk about? Wasn't it things that *they* needed to do? How important do you think the *one on one* time that Joe spent with his team was? Coaching and nurturing employees was apparently some of Joe's subtler, behind the scenes, leadership behaviors that Mary Beth didn't quite understand when she took over as manager. The importance of those subtle behaviors as they relate to building a bond of understanding, concern and caring by the manager for his staff should never be underestimated. How might employees interpret Mary Beth's example? Could it be that, "You care more about yourself, your work or the company than you do about me?"

B.) *Stealing "Gratification Income" from employees.*

When Mary Beth went into the field, saved the deal and then told the story did she help her sales rep to develop and gain the glory of success, or did she steal the glory for herself? From the sales reps perspective, what could Mary Beth's behavior imply about her level of confidence or trust in this sales rep? Her behavior suggested that she lacked both confidence and trust in the rep. Might not only he, but others begin to believe that she lacks confidence in them? They may also think she is selfish when they hear the stories of her conquests around the office. Over time, this could diminish the bonds of trust between Mary Beth and her people. How might employees interpret this example? Could it be that, "You don't really care about me. You care about making yourself look good?"

C.) *Holding End of the Month Crunch "pump up" meetings.*

Mary Beth seemed to believe that the meetings that she had seen Joe hold in past situations were in themselves powerful and motivating. You and I know that she was wrong, don't we? Most likely, the reason that these meetings were motivational when Joe held them is because he had exhibited the behind the scenes behaviors that built trust, commitment and understanding with the individual staff members before bringing them together as a group. I'm afraid that sometimes managers believe that the *RA-RA* meeting is leadership. Leadership is not in the meeting; it's in other things that occur before and after the meeting. How might employees interpret this example? Could it be that, "You don't really care about me, you just want me to hit *your* objectives?"

D.) *Facing her perceived threats to the team head on.*

Was it the team who was feeling threatened or was it Mary Beth's authority? Authority, like leadership is *earned* not *owed*. Mary Beth's biggest mistake was making the assumption that because senior management had given her a sales manager's job her people's desire to follow her would come with the job. She didn't seem to understand that the team's behavior might be the consequence of her behavior. First she must earn their respect as a person, not as a manager of procedure or as a closer, and then lead. By confronting the team without understanding or confronting her own issues, she *widens* the gap between herself and the team. How might employees interpret this example? Could it be that, "You don't really care about how we feel. You only care about how you feel?"

Do you see a trend in the possible perceptions and interpretations of Mary Beth's staff? Mary Beth's idea of leadership is a common one. She appeared to believe that leadership is about what you can get others to do. In true reality, *Leadership is about what you can get yourself to do!*

Real leadership is this: If you become great at anything that other people admire, they'll follow you whether you ask them to or not. That's leadership! If in your consistent behavior, you show them that you truly care about them and not only for yourself, then many of them and maybe all of them will stick around for a while and do the best that they can to help you achieve success for each staff member, the team and the company. They do that because they respect and admire you. They respect and admire what you've become as a person, and because of what your capable of as a developer, a mentor, a coach, and a leader. Most importantly, they follow you because they want to! That's why it's so important to ask yourself, *"By what example do I lead?"*

If you want good people to follow you, then you must set good examples. Poor examples bring poor staff or no staff, if everyone believes that they are better than you. This doesn't mean that if you're a sales manager, you are supposed to be the best sales person on the team, or that if you're a service manager, you're supposed to be some kind of *super-tech*. There are other examples that are much more important to an effective and powerful leader.

Let's see if this exercise will bring the points of this chapter home for you.

Exercise: Leadership Characteristics

Think of someone that you've followed in the past. Make it someone who you respected, trusted and followed. It could be a previous boss, parent, mentor, teacher or coach. It could be anyone in your life who you respected, trusted and followed. Now, answer the following question with as many answers as possible.

What Characteristics did this person possess that you respected? *(Examples of Characteristics could include: Decisive, Caring, Motivating, Honest, etc…)*

1.)_____   6.) _____

2.)_____   7.) _____

3.)_____   8.) _____

4.)_____   9.) _____

5.)_____   10.) _____

How do you feel about your list? How many of the characteristics that you listed would you consider to be *internal values*? Do you remember now why this person was or is so important to you? Isn't their importance to you and your willingness to follow them connected in some way to the internal values that this person possesses? By the way, aren't internal values things that we ask ourselves to do? Internal values rules and expectations that we ask ourselves to live by.

Is the leadership light beginning to come on in your head now? Many of you may have already understood what I'm explaining about leadership, but if you didn't, I hope that the characteristics of true leadership are beginning to take shape and make more common sense.

Here's another question: if the reasons that you respected and followed this person were because of their internal values, then how did you see them? If they were *internal*, then what did you see or experience *externally* that convinced you that this person possessed these values? Most likely, it was the behavior of the person that demonstrated the values. The way we truly feel, the true priorities that we possess, and our internal values affect the way that we make decisions and ultimately act!

Then if it is our desire to become the best possible leader we must do three things:

Three Leadership Steps:

1.) *Identify Leadership Characteristics that you respect and wish to "internalize."*

In the previous exercise you created a list of characteristics that you respected in someone that you've followed. Isn't that a good place to start? Go back to that list and put a *star* next to the characteristics that you believe you already possess and exhibit. Then, *circle* those characteristics that you would like to internalize in the future.

2.) *Identify the Behaviors that best exhibit those Characteristics.*

What things did this person do that showed you that they possessed the characteristics that you've chosen to internalize? Can you do the same things? If not, what can you do? *(Example: Caring = A good listener.)*

Exercise: Identifying Future Behavior

What are the Characteristics that I wish to internalize and what behaviors can I exhibit everyday that will help me to do so?

Characteristics: **What will I do?**

1.) _____   _____
                                              _____

2.) _____   _____
                                              _____

3.) _____   _____
                                              _____

4.) _____   _____
                                              _____

5.) _____   _____
                                              _____

3.) *Commit to living those behaviors.*

Remember, you didn't get the way you are over night. You got the way you are over time. If you're going to change the way you are you should be *optimistically patient* with yourself and allow time to grow and develop your new characteristics and behaviors. Now that I've softened the blow…make the choice. Are you willing to commit to the characteristics that you know the leaders that you respected and followed possessed? If so, then make the commitment. A true commitment is: *Doing what you said that you would do, long after the mood that you said it in has passed!* So if you want to be the kind of leader that I know every person is capable of, then commit to living your chosen behaviors.

Conclusions:

Leadership has always been about what we can get ourselves to do, not others. You may have already known that. Whenever we commit ourselves to being the very best that we can be at anything, then people who appreciate that best will want to be near us, and follow us. Consider sports figures, spiritual leaders, politicians, rock stars, environmental or political activists all of these people can be leaders. I'm not suggesting that any of these people possess all of the characteristics that you or I would think that a great leader should possess. Although some of them may. What I *am* suggesting is that whenever you focus your time, talents, attention and efforts in order to become the very best at anything, people that respect those efforts and results will want to follow in your footsteps and take your direction. That's leadership!

Leadership has never been about charisma, personality, or birthright. Leadership is all about us deciding what behaviors are best for our self and our staff, customers, company and loved ones. Then we must commit ourselves at the highest possible level to become the very best that we can be at internalizing the appropriate values, then externalizing our chosen decisions and behaviors. Could becoming the world's greatest *people developer* and *relationship builder* provide the following of staff members that you may be looking for on your team?

Remember: *True character is doing what you believe to be right…even when no one else is watching or when no one else will ever know!* That's also the true essence of leadership, and that's an example that people will want to follow. And why shouldn't they? It's the right thing to do.

Chapter Thirteen

Successful Implementation Strategy

Congratulations and thank you for taking the time to read this little book. You've certainly taken the first steps toward improving decision-making by reading and working your way through these pages. You've proven your commitment to better management, leadership and to your team! Bravo!

Even though the strategies contained in these pages is only a small part of what we offer in workshops, it may still be a considerable amount to digest and more importantly to implement for some managers. Should you be a new manager who's looking for a successful decision-making process and style, or a tenured manager who's simply looking to make current world adjustments and additions to your already successful decision-making *tool kit*, these pages are here for you.

The responsibilities of management and leadership are greater today than they have ever been. And, according to the men and women with whom I've had the fortunate pleasure to work over the years, with great responsibility, can come great reward.

The satisfaction at the end of the day knowing that you made the right decision, at the right time, and for the right reasons is one reward. The smile that you get from a staff member when you've helped one to become more than they ever though possible is another. Becoming the contributing *heart* of a true high performance team where everyone believes that "it just doesn't get any better than this!" is a feeling that can't be described, only experienced. I wish with all my heart for you to experience these and all of the other incredible rewards of great management and leadership. You are no doubt well on your way to achieving them.

Some of you may be thinking, "Thanks Kim…that sounds wonderful…but what do I do first?" Don't worry. I'm not going to bail out on you so close to the goal line of achievement. We need to talk about *implementation*.

Successful implementation begins with one important understanding. **You are already successful!** Have I mentioned that? I believe that I did. You are already successful, so take stock of your success. No doubt, when you read through this little book you found some decisions, attitudes or techniques that you were already using effectively. Maybe there was one thing, maybe there were ten, but you no doubt found some or thought of some by reading and working your way through the book. You should do is to recognize yourself for the things that you do well.

Exercise: Step One – Celebrate Success!

What things did I discover by reading this book that I do well?

(Review your notes and work in these pages and answer this question. Some of the topics and strategies of this book may have affirmed things that you already do well; what are they? Write them down.)

1.) _____

2.) _____

3.) _____

4.) _____

5.) _____

(You may have found more than five things to write down. If so, don't leave them out, write them down so you can appreciate and nurture your successes.)

Exercise: Step Two – Choose Your Improvement Opportunities!

Answer this question: Of the attitudes, strategies and techniques in this book, which ones do I feel I need to implement?

(Take time to review. Considering the topics and strategies offered in this book which one(s) do you feel might benefit you and/or your team. Make a list of the chapters that you believe you should focus on in the future. Write down the attitude, strategy or technique that you wish to apply. Then list the possible benefits of improving your decision-making ability or quality in this area of management/ leadership.)

Chapter #: Attitude, Strategy, Technique:		Benefits:

Step Three – Create Your Improvement Plan

There are two rules to creating and implementing a successful self-improvement plan.

<u>Rule # 1: Go Slow! Prioritize Improvement.</u>

Sometimes we have to slow down to make significant impact on personal improvement. If a person attempts to change too many things, too quickly in their behavior or decision style often none of the changes will last. So…go slow!

Exercise: Prioritize Improvement

Go back to the previous exercise where you listed the chapters that you'd like to focus on for improvement and then *stack rank* and number them based on your desire to implement that approach and/or achieve your desired outcomes. Which do you think would be most important for you and your team? Which would be next? And so on…

Once you've *stack ranked* your improvement opportunities, look at the ones that you have numbered *one* and *two*. Consider working on those until you feel that you have comfortably mastered them and then pick one or two more to work on. You shouldn't work on more than one or two per month. Remember, we change *over time*.

Rule # 2: Be Optimistically Patient with Yourself!

We each have decision-making habits. It may take time and more than one active strategy and planned approach to completely change the way you think, make decisions and act. Cut yourself some slack! Be optimistically patient with yourself. If the change in you is important enough to you, it will come over time. Be patient. Stay focused. Review your plans. Review the benefits of changing and most importantly; remember that you've accomplished what you have in business because of the good that you done, so stay positive as you make your changes.

I hope that this approach and this book may help you to reach the level of decision-making quality that you desire. I know that that the strategies in this little book are proven to work. Successful men and women helped to develop these strategies, believe in them and use them. The managers that have added these or similar strategies and decision-making approaches into their already successful working styles are very pleased with the results that they've produced. I believe that each of you have the ability to achieve the same.

To manage and lead others is an honor and a challenge. We are honored with the opportunity and challenged by almost everyone we come in contact with for the appropriate decisions.

I don't know what you may need. I don't know what you may want. Maybe it's fewer fires, more productive people, less headaches, higher levels of achievement by your team, a ten-hour workday instead of twelve; I don't know what those things that you want are, but I do know this… *"If you want something that you've never had…you'll probably need to do something that you've never done!"* So you'll most likely need to consider changing!

Thank you again for taking the time to read these pages and your ongoing commitment to excellence as a manager and leader of people. I wish for you blessings, happiness, good relationships and results!

About the Author

Kim D. Ward is the founder of *Outsource Training Solutions* whose home office is in Orlando, Florida. He has been involved in the training and consulting industry in a variety of capacities since 1990. His expertise encompasses training needs analysis and assessment, business/ process reorganization, consulting, curriculum development, keynote speaking, training, and facilitation. Kim has been instrumental in helping numerous organizations achieve and exceed sales growth and profitability objectives. He has authored and co-authored numerous training programs including *Leading High Velocity Change* and *C3 Partnering for Success*.

As a lecturer/ facilitator Kim has delivered hundreds of workshops to thousands of participants all over the world. His professional presence, personal success and ability to engage his audience has earned him an excellent reputation in several industries including communications, technology and e-commerce, automotive, office automation and distribution, banking, real estate and others.

Kim has over 25 years of sales, management, and executive leadership experience. He is a member of numerous civic and professional organizations and resides with his family in Longwood, Florida.

To obtain additional copies of this book:
<u>*www.outsourcetrainingsolutions.com*</u>
or
To discuss your specific training needs:

contact us at:

1-800-403-9379

0-595-25866-2

Lightning Source UK Ltd.
Milton Keynes UK
09 October 2010

160984UK00001B/51/A